BRANTFORD PUBLIC LIBRARY
39154900016676

D0851773

*Summers
in Supino*

Summers in Supino

BECOMING ITALIAN

a memoir

MARIA COLETTA McLEAN

ECW Press

Copyright © Maria Coletta McLean, 2013

Published by ECW Press
2120 Queen Street East, Suite 200, Toronto, Ontario, Canada M4E 1E2
416-694-3348 / info@ecwpress.com

All rights reserved. No part of this publication may be reproduced, stored in a retrieval system, or transmitted in any form by any process — electronic, mechanical, photocopying, recording, or otherwise — without the prior written permission of the copyright owners and ECW Press. The scanning, uploading, and distribution of this book via the Internet or via any other means without the permission of the publisher is illegal and punishable by law. Please purchase only authorized electronic editions, and do not participate in or encourage electronic piracy of copyrighted materials. Your support of the author's rights is appreciated.

Library and Archives Canada Cataloguing in Publication

McLean, Maria Coletta, 1946–
Summers in Supino : becoming Italian : a memoir / Maria
Coletta McLean.

ISBN 978-1-77041-137-1
Also issued as: 978-1-77090-363-0 (PDF); 978-1-77090-364-7 (ePUB)

1. McLean, Maria Coletta, 1946– —Travel—Italy—Supino.
2. Supino (Italy)—Biography. 3. Supino (Italy)—Description
and travel. I. Title.

DG692.M35 2013   914.56'220492   C2012-907509-4

Cover and text design: Tania Craan
Cover image: © Ron Watts/Corbis
Author photo: John Carvalho, Exposures Photography
Printing: Friesens 5 4 3 2 1

The publication of *Summers in Supino* has been generously supported by the Canada Council for the Arts which last year invested $20.1 million in writing and publishing throughout Canada, and by the Ontario Arts Council, an agency of the Government of Ontario. We also acknowledge the financial support of the Government of Canada through the Canada Book Fund for our publishing activities, and the contribution of the Government of Ontario through the Ontario Book Publishing Tax Credit. The marketing of this book was made possible with the support of the Ontario Media Development Corporation.

Printed and bound in Canada

The moment I met Bob McLean, my heart began to beat more joyously, and over the years this has never changed, so this book's for you, Bob:

ti amo, per sempre.

One

The news of my father's death came flying over the ocean and sped down the *autostrada* until it reached the blue sign pointing to Supino, his village. Here it slowed, as it climbed the curves and hills, weaving through the beech trees that arched over the roadway leading to the ancient church of San Sebastiano. The melancholy news rang from the bell tower. It arrived in wicker baskets along with the winter vegetables, it unfolded from the January news, and was carried in patched pockets jingling among the coins to be exchanged at the market and the bakery and the *tabacchi* store. In the January dusk, the wind carried his name beyond the village and up the mountain path to Santa Serena, where the cows stopped momentarily to listen before they lowered their bony heads and continued grazing on the wild sage. High above the mountaintops, his name, Loreto, put down roots among the clouds.

Every activity had lost its appeal since my father's death and I'd been hesitant about returning to our little house in Supino. We'd spent 10 sunny days there with my father last August. But since he had died in the winter of 1992, I was worried that our future visits to his village would remain in the shadow of sorrow.

When I explained my concerns to Bob, he said Supino was *our* village too, and we had a lifetime to make new memories there. "As soon as we drive up the main street, you'll get excited to be back," Bob said. "Supino's always good for you."

He called our neighbour, Joe, who lived across the street on *via condotto vecchio*. Joe and his wife, Angela, looked after our house when we weren't there. I overheard Bob confirming our plans: "*Sì*, July. *Sì*, Sunday. *Sì*, afternoon. *Sì*, rental car." At the end of the conversation, Bob's voice grew uncertain even though he kept repeating, "*Sì, sì,*" and finally, "*Arrivederci.*"

He put down the phone. "It's all set."

"Everything's okay?"

"Sure. In fact, Joe has a surprise for you. He said to tell you that he repainted the house."

It took me a moment to realize that Joe meant our house. I thought about our next-door neighbour Peppe. He'd painted his house orange last summer. Said it was a warm colour.

"Did he mention the colour?"

"He talked mostly about his son, Marco — he got a job at a factory outside Supino on that road that runs parallel to the *autostrada*."

"He didn't say he painted it orange, did he?"

"No. The government divided half the jobs among workers from the South and half from the North. So a few Northerners are boarding at the *pensione* just outside of the village."

"Do you think he repainted it white? Just to freshen it up?"

"He didn't say. Let me finish. When Joe found out how much the workers were paying to stay at the *pensione*, he said that Angela could feed them better for half the price and . . . well . . . here's the thing — the workers are boarding at our house."

"At *our* house? Bob, for heaven's sake. What did you say?"

"What *could* I say?"

Bob was right. Whatever he said, Joe would have said, "Don't worry about it." If there was one thing we'd learned about owning a little house in my father's village of Supino, it was that it was always better to go along with the villagers and their traditions. Joe could speak English and he looked after our house when we weren't there. "I keep an eye," was how Joe explained it; that meant he kept the house and its contents and the tiny backyard the way he liked it. So what if our furniture was often rearranged to suit his wife's taste? So what if odd bits of furnishings, like a wardrobe, a folding table, and a stool with a broken leg, found their way into our house? So what if our tiny back garden was full of Joe's brother's plants?

The important thing was that when we called each summer to say we were coming to Supino, our house was always spotless. When we left, we simply gathered our bed sheets and towels and left them for Angela, along with an envelope of euros on the kitchen table, and when we returned everything was washed and dried and folded in wooden crates that Joe had gathered for us to use as a linen closet. If something went wrong at the house, like the water pump wouldn't work, we told Joe and he fixed it or brought in someone who could, and another envelope of euros would change hands.

Joe knew everything that was going on in the village, he knew everyone who lived in the village, he carried the keys for all four churches in Supino in his pocket — so our house key was safe among them.

Six months after my father's death, on a hot July afternoon, we arrived in Supino. Outside the Kennedy Bar, men were playing cards as usual, scaffolding still surrounded the proposed Supino old folks home, the Bar Italia was closed, and an ice cream truck was parked in the middle of the street, blocking the corner of *via d'Italia* and *via condotto vecchio*. We stopped our rental car, and Cristina, from the *tabacchi* store, opened the passenger door.

"Mi dispiace," she said, reaching in to hug me. I was to hear that phrase, "I'm sorry," over and over during the next few days. Every villager we passed repeated those words to us until I thought I couldn't bear to hear them anymore.

Up the hill to number 10 *via condotto vecchio*, we climbed, with a suitcase in each hand, saying, *"Buongiorno,"* to every face at every window, while I wondered what colour Joe had painted our house and how many factory workers might be living there.

But the house was still white, and no strangers lounged on our verandah. However, the front door was wide open and rock music blared from a radio inside. Peering into our doorway, we saw a stranger's sweater hung over the back of our chair, a package of Marlboro cigarettes and a tangle of keys waiting on our table. We set our bags down and followed the music up the newly washed stairs.

"You come already," declared Angela from the second floor. "Marco, hurry up. Move the broom. Shut that noise. Sorry. *Scusa*. Bob, Maria, *mi dispiace*. Your father — a good man."

We looked around for signs of the factory workers, but there was only Angela and her son, Marco.

"Marco," said Bob, "your dad tells me you're working."

"No more. Finished last week."

"Marco," said Angela, "hurry up. Let Bob and Maria rest. Get out of the way. Go. Take that noise with you. Go, go."

Two minutes later, our house was empty, just the echo of Angela's voice as she called up the stairs, "Come later to eat. Sleep now."

When Bob carried up our suitcases, he held an envelope of euros in his hand. "Our share of the boarders' rent money," he explained. "And by the way, someone's drunk all the brandy from the wooden cabinet."

We lay down on sheets that smelled like fresh air and sunshine, and there above the bed, on the freshly painted ceiling, was the chandelier from the living room. Joe must have moved it. I thought about going down to see what light fixture he'd hung downstairs, but, really, what was the point? I closed my eyes and slept.

I dreamt the same dream I'd had since my father's death six months before. It was the day of my aunt Reg and uncle Fidel's 50th wedding anniversary. The celebration was in September, just a week after we'd returned from Supino with my father. Dad had lined up at the buffet table and piled his dish high with all the foods my mother said he wasn't allowed to eat. When my mother objected, he'd dismissed her complaints with a wave of his hand: "It's a party. I eat what I want tonight." Everyone said how good Dad looked; he'd gained 10 pounds and a lot of his confidence during our 10 days in Supino. My dad and I had danced together that night, laughing as he wove me in and out between the other couples, circling around the floor, breathless by the time the music stopped. I'd forgotten what a good dancer my father was, so light on his feet, so sure of his steps.

In December, my dad suffered a burst aneurysm. Bob called an ambulance and on the way to the hospital I phoned my brother and sister. Within the hour we were in the emergency waiting room. I gave my father's name, Loreto Coletta, and the nurse said, "They're preparing him for surgery."

When my father had first been diagnosed with the aneurysm a few months earlier, the doctor had advised him that if he didn't have the operation, the aneurysm would continue to grow and eventually it would burst; surgery at that point would be less successful. My father had said, "I'll take my chances."

We talked about the emergency surgery, reassuring each other that the doctors could repair the aneurysm. Then the doctor arrived. "There's a problem," he said. "We've prepared your father for surgery. We can repair the aneurysm but we don't think he'll survive the operation. What do you want to do? Every minute we wait decreases his chances of survival. He's paralyzed and can't speak for himself."

"Can't speak . . ." I began.

The doctor said, "You can speak to him. He'll hear you."

We discussed the options. Our father was a fighter but he was also 83. He might die on the operating table. And if we didn't do anything, he'd die. What would he want us to do? We asked the doctor what Dad's chances were.

"Not good," he said. "There's his age, and he's already lost a lot of blood. What do you want to do?"

"He wouldn't want to die on the operating table," I said. "He'd want his family around him."

So we said no to the operation and left the waiting room to sit with our father. A nurse pulled the white curtain around his bed.

Dad's pale blue eyes were bright, but his colour had faded away. I could hear his breath coming slower and slower. As I stood beside his bed, his cool hand in mine, I did not speak about the burst aneurysm or the surgery. I said, "We're here, Dad. We're all here with you."

"In Supino," I added, repeating the words my father had told me all my life, "it's wintertime, but there's no snow. Just cold. Your mother would be knitting woolen caps and socks for Christmas. Your father would have saved some filberts from the autumn harvest to roast along with the chestnuts for the Christmas Eve feast. There'd be figs stuffed with walnuts and rolled in honey . . ."

My father died on the first night of December. The Toronto streets were illuminated with festive lights, the store windows decorated for the holidays. When I saw them, I was a little surprised the holidays hadn't been cancelled.

That Christmas, Bob gave me a small box as dark as a blue Supino sky. Gold letters spelled out the name of the jewellery store in my father's village. Inside was a pair of gold earrings. "Your dad helped me pick them out last summer," said Bob.

From here on, our lives would always be divided by that December, by the days before my father died and the days after.

Two

In Supino, we always started our day with a walk down our street to the Bar Italia for cappuccino. Last year, when my father was with us, we came to the Bar Italia on the first morning and sat outside on the little patio and drank cappuccino. Bob and Dad, who both had a sweet tooth, ate croissants or *cornettos*, little tubes of flaky pastry filled with cream. But when Bob went to pay, Bianca, the owner, shook her head. As Bob double-checked the bills to be sure he was giving the right amount, my father explained that Bianca wouldn't accept payment because it was our first day in the village. Bob tried to insist, but my father said, "Think of it as a welcome-home gift."

By the second day, the news of my father's return had circulated throughout the village, and after that, people from his past joined us every morning. Old school friends, neighbours, distant relatives, and the curious: they all stopped by to say hello and welcome us back, and inevitably when Bob went to pay, someone else had already done so. My father had an expression I'd heard all my life — "That's the way it is." And I came to understand its meaning in Supino. There was no arguing — well, you could if you wanted to, but it wouldn't make any difference. This is how things are done in Supino and, therefore, "That's the way it is."

Today, as we walked to the bar, Bob carried a road map of Italy tucked under his arm. I wanted to drive down to Vietri sul Mare, a small village in southern Italy where the artisans specialized in hand-painted ceramics. I planned to buy some new tiles for the kitchen of our Supino house. Joe had plastered some spare maroon tiles behind the kitchen sink, but he was short a couple so he'd filled the last corner with a few small black-and-white tiles that were left over from a bathroom renovation. "All free," Joe had pointed out as he polished off the dusty grout.

Like my father, Joe saw no need to spend money for new if you could use what you already had. I was going to buy some bright and beautiful tiles from Vietri sul Mare and figure out how to rationalize the expense to Joe once I had them in hand. I'd stress that the tiles were from my mother's province of Campania. "Sentiment might override economics just this once," I told Bob, and he told me I was kidding myself. When I'd mentioned to Rocco, our Toronto travel agent, that we planned to buy some ceramics, he had told us to contact his partner, Pietro, in Supino for directions to Vietri sul Mare. Apparently Pietro had a cousin who owned a shop there.

"Go to the Kennedy Bar on Sunday morning, about 11," Rocco told us. "Pietro will be there."

"How will we know him?"

Rocco shrugged, made a circular motion with his hand, like swiftly sweeping crumbs toward himself from an invisible table. "Look around," he said.

After our cappuccino, and after Bob had spread the map on the metal table and traced the route from Supino to Vietri sul Mare, he said, "It's almost 11. We'd better head down to the Kennedy Bar and look for Pietro."

"I think Rocco used the expression *around 11*, which probably means sometime about noon. We'll just be standing there for an hour."

"So, I'll buy you an ice cream."

"What's the word for strawberry?" Bob asked as we stood in front of the ice cream counter at the Kennedy Bar.

A voice from the crowd responded, "Ahh, you speak English," and a man in a coal-black suit stepped forward and stretched out his hand to shake ours.

"Hello, I'm Bob McLean."

"And I'm Maria Coletta . . ."

"Ahh, the family of *Mezzabotte*," he said, using the family nickname. "How is your father, Maria?"

I stopped, mouth open, frozen. Tears jumped to my eyelids.

Bob said, "He died in December."

"I'm so sorry. *Mi dispiace* . . ."

It was as if I was hearing it all again for the first time. The doctors in the emergency room saying, "Sorry, he's dead." The ambulance driver telling me, "Sorry." The nurse, the priest, the orderlies: "Sorry, sorry, sorry." I was angry at them all, angry at death. I was even angry with this stranger for not knowing.

"I didn't hear. I've been travelling — tours to France, to . . . But excuse me. Permit me to introduce myself. I am Pietro, partner of Rocco, your travel agent."

Pietro listened to our plan to travel down the Amalfi Coast, nodding his head to everything we said.

"When do you want to go?"

"We thought we'd head down there tomorrow," I said.

"Impossible. Just this moment I was talking to Franco, who tells me his father-in-law is here from Toronto, so of course, I will take you to Franco's house for lunch tomorrow."

"I don't . . ."

"Don't worry, Maria. They all speak English."

"I don't know Franco —"

"Your cousin Suzy's husband, Johnny, grew up in that same section of Supino as Franco. They went to school together. There used to be a butcher shop near the corner, right beside the fruit store and . . ."

Later, I said to Bob, "We have to be careful about these invitations. I know Pietro means well, inviting us to his friend's house to meet his friend's wife's father or whatever, but that can easily lead to another invitation to another dinner with some other friend, and before you know it, our vacation will be over and we won't have had time to do anything but go from one house to another to eat a meal."

"What's wrong with that?" said Bob. "We have to eat anyway."

Bob had grown up in a family of four; his parents ran a little grocery store six days a week and the family had gone out for the traditional roast beef dinner every Sunday night to give his mother a break from cooking. Even after they sold the grocery store on Caledonia Road, moved to the town of Weston, and bought a coffee-roasting plant where Bob had been working for the past three years, they continued to go out for dinner on the weekends. My family never went to a restaurant. On Sunday, we might go to a relative's house where there'd be a raft of other relatives and we'd all be crammed around tables talking, laughing, and eating. Or some relatives would come to our house.

The first time I invited Bob to come for Sunday dinner, he brought flowers for my mother. We didn't have a vase; my aunt had to go downstairs to her place and find one, and there was a discussion about whether to cut the ends off the flowers or just put them in the way they were. While that debate was going on in the kitchen, I took Bob into the living room and introduced him around: my dad, my brother, my sister-in-law, my nephew, my sister, my sister's boyfriend, my cousins . . . Partway around the room, we had to detour around the dining room table, which had been pulled out to its full length and now protruded into the living room like a small peninsula. Bob stuck a couple of fingers underneath his shirt collar and wiggled it a little.

I said, "Don't worry. You don't have to remember everyone's name."

"Are these *all* your cousins?" he asked.

"Of course not. These cousins just dropped in on their way up north. Usually there's only about a dozen of us for dinner. Tonight's a bit of an exception. Do you have a lot of cousins?"

"I have three," he said.

"I have about 33."

The dinner conversation began with counting cousins — did we have 33 or more? — and that led to heated discussions about cousins living in Italy and the States and whether we were including them in the count. We ate my mother's homemade ravioli and drank Uncle Primo's homemade wine. The meatballs sparked a lively discussion between my two aunts regarding the addition of ground pork and veal to the ground beef and whether the extra expense was worth it. A third debate took off from there concerning Romano cheese — should it be added to the meatball mixture before cooking or just sprinkled on afterwards?

Then I brought in the salad and my brother taught Bob his "secret method" of cutting a meatball in half and using it to wipe the spaghetti sauce off his plate so that the plate was cleaned for the salad. The salad was already dressed with oil and Uncle Primo's wine from last year that had turned to vinegar. Bob was asking why we ate our salad after our meal and what were these dark leaves — escarole, we explained. And he missed most of the argument about who made the best wine in the family. I brought in the chocolate cake my mother had made; my sister brought the coffee pot. By the time the plates and cups had been filled and distributed around the table, there were a dozen different conversations going on and I realized Bob had given up trying to keep track and was sitting back, like my dad, just watching.

I went to the McLeans' house for dinner the following

week. We sat in the living room, among freshly polished end tables adorned with starched lace doilies and vases of porcelain flowers. To get to the couch I had to walk across an Indian carpet with visible vacuum marks and see my footsteps once I sat down. Bob's parents asked me about school. I was in my final year at Weston Collegiate and I started talking about *Wuthering Heights*. I thought it was going pretty well until I realized they were talking about the movie and I was talking about the book.

At the dinner table, we began with iceberg lettuce quarters in individual wooden bowls. On the table were bottles of salad dressing I'd never heard of before — blue cheese, Thousand Island, and ranch. Then Mr. McLean passed me a plate with a slice of rare roast beef and asked, "Horseradish?"

I had no idea what he was talking about until Bob reached over and offered me a bowl filled with grated something that smelled sharp and looked anemic. "No, thank you," I said.

Mrs. McLean passed me another bowl containing another pale condiment. "Sour cream? For your baked potato?"

"No, thank you."

After that, no one spoke; they just ate. Partway through the meal, someone passed a small plate of Wonder Bread slices and a smaller bowl of butter. I thought back to our dinner table with crusty buns, fresh from the Italian bakery, piled on the tablecloth, and one plate per person. Here, there were multiple plates and silverware and everything matched. Our table settings were as diverse as the company who squeezed around the table, talking and laughing. Here, everything was peaceful and orderly. I got so unnerved by the silence that I forgot to eat my foil-wrapped baked potato waiting in its own little wicker basket to the left of my bread-and-butter plate.

"Did you not like your potato?" asked Bob's mother.

I assured her I had just overlooked it and they sat and waited silently while I ate my potato. Sweat gathered under my armpits, erupted across my forehead, as I forked pieces of a potato the size of P.E.I. into my mouth. For dessert we had a store-bought apple pie. Bob's mother cut the pie and started putting large slices on the dessert plates. While I was trying to think of a polite way to say I couldn't eat that much pie, Bob's father was offering me cream for my coffee, so I said, "No, thank you. Not for me." As a result, I had no cream and no pie. I was left to choke down bitter black coffee while they ate their pie and drank their coffee with sweet cream.

I never did get used to his family's quiet Sunday dinners, but Bob enjoyed the boisterous gatherings at my house and my relatives' homes. He embraced the Italian tradition of celebrating every family occasion with a big meal and a big crowd.

The morning after our meeting with Pietro, we were sitting outside the Bar Italia watching the market-day activities when a man appeared at our table.

"Mr. Bob of Toronto?" asked the stranger. "*Buongiorno*. Good morning. I'm Franco. Ahh, Maria, your father. *Mi dispiace* . . . I was knocking on your door and one of your neighbours called out, 'Bar Italia,' so here I am. I'm taking you for lunch."

"I think Pietro's coming for us later," I said.

"Change of plans," said Franco.

"Will you have a coffee?" asked Bob, because it was barely
11 o'clock and way too early for the one o'clock lunch, but
Franco declined. He said we had to get going, and since his
Fiat was parked half on the road, half on the patio of the
bar, we got in immediately.

As we sped off, Franco said he was taking us on a little
pre-lunch sightseeing trip to the town of Anagni. "Just a few
kilometres away," he assured us. Bob and I settled back in
our seats; we knew that a few Italian kilometres could mean
five or could mean 60.

Anagni turned out to be like a lot of the villages in the
area — first you had to drive back and forth across the face of
the mountain before you reached the town. There were the
same cobblestone streets, some too narrow for cars, others
stuffed with Fiats and Vespas and stray dogs, the lines of
laundry crisscrossing the roadways, the red geraniums tumbling from the window boxes, the market vendors set up in
the piazza. We stopped at a cathedral set high on the hillside
to enjoy the view.

"Look there," instructed Franco, "at the base of the
mountain. That's Supino."

The cathedral itself was closed for repairs, so we couldn't
see the frescoes Franco told us covered the walls and ceilings.
Instead we went to a little shop nearby that sold postcards.
After we'd admired those, we stepped into the bar next door
and had a cappuccino.

"Even though the cathedral is closed," Franco assured
us, "this is one of the finest views of Supino." As if it was

worth the drive to this village, just to admire the place we'd started out from. Then Franco checked his watch. "Time to pick up my daughter. My wife wants me to also pick up a loaf of bread from the bakery."

We jumped back in the Fiat and just outside of Supino we slowed near the intersection of the four streets, *Quattro Strade*. Franco pulled into the empty gravel parking lot of a dark, deserted-looking building. No lights and no sign. I could just hear Joe: *What you need a sign for? Everybody knows it's the bakery.*

The bakery was an unfinished room containing plaster pails, wheelbarrows, and deserted tubs of water. In the corner three workers were unwrapping their lunches and the fragrance of roasted peppers scented the air. Franco got involved in their discussion of the first figs of the season. The next thing we knew he was holding a glass of wine.

"Vino?" offered one of the workers, but we shook our heads.

"We have to buy bread," I reminded Franco. "We have to pick up your daughter."

Franco turned to the workers and gestured with an upturned palm. *"Canadese,"* he explained, but he downed the wine, shook hands all round, and headed to the door.

We followed Franco into a back room that boasted a wooden floor, rare in Italy, where most floors are marble. There was a highly polished oak bar with wooden barstools, wooden saloon doors, and heavy oak tables with matching chairs. Posters for cowboy movies covered the walls. No bread in sight.

"The owner likes cowboys, especially John Wayne," Franco explained. "He's opening a Western-style restaurant serving American hamburgers and hot dogs and beer. Also a karaoke machine. Grand opening in August. How long are you staying, Bob?"

"We're heading down the coast tomorrow . . ."

"Tomorrow's the dinner at Alberto's house. Pietro told me he's picking you up at seven o'clock. Sharp. Like Canadian time. Alberto's acquired this North American habit of punctuality."

"Wait a minute," I said. "We don't know anyone named Alberto. Why do you think we're going to his house?"

"Dinner," explained Franco.

Before I could continue my questions, Franco had opened another door, and we walked into a room heavy with the scent of freshly baked bread. No bakers, no cashier, not even a cash register. Franco stuffed some euros into a bat-tered tin sitting on the windowsill, grabbed two long loaves off the rack, and we roared off to pick up his daughter.

In the schoolyard, children in coloured smocks played among the tranquil grey nuns. Franco's daughter was dressed in a blue gingham smock with tiny roses embroidered across the bodice. Her black curls bounced as she ran toward us: *"Papà, papà."* As we drove to their house, the little girl, Adriana, tucked herself in beside me, resting her head against my arm.

Franco lived just outside of town, where the newer homes had been built on large lots. He pointed out his neigh-bours' homes as we drove along: "Your travel agent Rocco's summer home. The mayor's house. Pietro's house." As we pulled into a driveway paved with interlocking pink stones, Franco added, "Pietro tells me you are a councillor in Toronto, Bob. I'm a councillor here in Supino. You must tell me all about Canadian politics."

Franco opened the front door of his house with a little flourish and proceeded to give us a tour, with his wife apologizing all the way. Sorry, she hadn't had time to make fresh pasta, so Franco's mother had made the fettuccine for today's lunch; she hoped that was okay. Sorry, the dining room table was being refinished; it stood on a large white drop cloth, drowsy flecks of sawdust still drifting in the warm air — we must eat in the kitchen. Sorry, sorry. She hoped we wouldn't mind. On the balcony overlooking a ravine we drank sweet vermouth in stubby kitchen glasses. She apologized for them too. Her crystal was packed away until the dining room set was finished. Sorry.

In the garden below, an older man was throwing grain to the chickens. I thought of my father.

My parents had moved next door to us in Toronto, and after my father had turned his backyard into a vegetable garden, he made a suggestion for our yard. "We could put a few chickens back here," he said. "Make a chicken run and a coop."

"I don't think so, Dad," I said. "You can't really keep chickens in the city."

But my father didn't think in terms of Toronto by-laws; he still used Supinese logic. "Who's going to know?" he asked.

So, my dad and our 10-year-old son Ken built some chicken coops, attached them to the back of the garage, and fenced an area with chicken wire. There were no blueprints, building permits, or purchased construction materials involved because my dad believed in using whatever materials you already had or could get for free. That's why there were spare boards and leftover pieces of plywood stored in the garage; that's why Dad usually had a small ball of twine, a few nails, and his penknife in his pocket.

They started out with three chickens. The hens were all good layers and we usually had two fresh eggs each day. This supply of free eggs might have lasted longer if Ken hadn't wanted to take the chickens for a walk, as if they were pet dogs, and if my father hadn't shown Ken how to tie a piece of twine — which he conveniently had in his pocket — into a slipknot and slide it over the chicken's leg. Ken took the chickens for a walk on our adjoining front lawns so the hens had a good stretch of new ground to peck and scratch, and the neighbours had a good view of "livestock" kept within the city limits. When the letter arrived from the city by-law enforcement office, my father said we should just ignore it, but Bob assured him that we couldn't, so my father laid out our two options: eat the chickens or move them to my brother's farm 30 minutes north.

That weekend, Ken and my father dismantled the chicken coops and loaded them into the trunk, tucked the three chickens into a burlap sack, put it on the floor of the back seat, and drove to the farm.

Franco's wife joined us on the balcony and called down to her father — *"Papà!"* — and the man turned and lifted his hat. A few minutes later he came out onto the balcony as well. "I'm Giovanni. Call me John. Where do you live in Toronto?"

John and Bob talked about Toronto. John recommended a butcher on St. Clair, near where his family had lived. "Until my daughter married this man here and moved to Supino," he said, throwing his arm around Franco. "Look at this view. I told my wife we should move to Supino, but she likes the city life. She said, 'What am I going to do in Supino?' 'Same thing you do here,' I told her, but women want grocery stores and movie theatres and . . ."

We had roast chicken for lunch. I tried not to think about the chickens I'd just seen high-stepping in the yard. When the conversation had reached a lull, I asked, "Why are we invited to Alberto's house for dinner?"

Before anyone could answer, the mailman tapped at the kitchen shutter and held up a registered letter. Franco's wife motioned him inside: "You're late today."

With a nonchalant shrug, the mailman offered her a paper to sign. Franco's father-in-law squeezed over to make room at the table, and the mailman hung his bag on the back of the chair and reached for a bun.

"Finally," said Franco's wife as she tore open the envelope she'd signed for. "How many weeks have I been waiting for this?" She switched into Italian and her voice grew irritated as she read parts of the letter aloud.

Franco interrupted. "That's not what it means."

"Sure it does. It says right here —"

"Let me see." Franco took the letter; his wife snatched it back. Their voices grew louder.

Meanwhile the mailman was stuffing some chicken slices into a bun. "Put some lettuce," offered John, passing him the salad bowl. "You want some rapini?" He slid that bowl too toward the mailman, who loaded his bun, lifted his mailbag from the back of the chair, and headed for the door.

"*Grazie,*" he called, but the couple continued their argument without so much as an *arrivederci.*

I looked at Bob; maybe we should take our plates out to the balcony and let our hosts settle their fight in private?

Franco's wife jumped up from the table and jabbed her finger on the letter. "No, it says —"

"That's not what it means."

"This is formal Italian. You don't understand legal terms. All you know is Supinese dialect."

"Hey, I went to university. Do you think you know more than me just because you went to — ?"

"Of course."

"Basta." A sudden slam of Franco's fist on the tabletop. "That's enough."

Franco's wife turned and ran from the room. The door slammed. Franco raced after her. The door slammed again. Through the kitchen window I watched them running across the street, the letter shaking in Franco's wife's hand.

John picked up the wine bottle. "It's nothing," he said. "Some disagreement about the translation. The woman across the street is a *professore* at the university in Rome. She'll straighten it all out. *Vino?*"

After we finished our lunch with John, he turned on the element beneath the espresso pot, and when the coffee was gurgling, I poured it into the little cups waiting on the counter. John brought a box of pastries to the table. Thirty minutes passed without any sign of our hosts. John and Bob exchanged business cards and said they'd get together back in Toronto. I began to gather a few dishes, but John said, "Leave them. My daughter will do them when she returns." A few moments later, when he walked us to the door, he said, "Come again. Anytime." Our hosts had never returned.

As Bob and I started down the driveway to walk back to the village, Franco yelled out the neighbour's window, "*Ciao.* See you tomorrow night at Alberto's."

The street was bordered with blood-red poppies hanging their heads in the afternoon heat. "What a commotion over a translation," I said. "I wish she hadn't opened the letter while we were there."

"The professor will settle it," said Bob.

"And another thing. Who's Alberto and why are we going there for dinner tomorrow night? I want to go to Vietri."

"Joe said Alberto's a senator in Rome. I guess Pietro figures that since I'm on our city council, I'd like to meet Italian politicians."

"Pietro's a little pushy. First he tells us we're having lunch at Franco's — and we saw what a disaster that was — and now it's dinner at Alberto's. How'd he get to be in charge of our vacation?"

"He's just trying to be helpful. You said yourself that it's a Supinese tradition."

"Yes, but that's family or neighbours, not every Tom, Dick, and Pietro. At this rate, we'll never get to Vietri." I stopped to look at the unfamiliar landscape. "Where are we anyway?"

"We're almost at the Kennedy Bar," said Bob. "We'll be home in 20 minutes." After a few more steps, he said, "You know, we never walked in this section last year when your father was with us. He always headed up any street that led to the mountain where he used to live and where he walked his cow every morning. I guess he was following his old routine."

My dad always woke up early — when he lived in Supino

and walked his cow up the mountain, and later when he worked at Toronto Macaroni and delivered to small Italian grocery stores. He kept the early morning routine even after he retired. Bob was always up early too, because he helped the drivers load up at the coffee company where he worked. So, in Supino, Bob and my father had woken up early and gone out walking, Bob automatically matching his steps to my father's slower ones.

"What did you two talk about on those morning walks?" I asked Bob.

"Nothing special," he said. "Your father's usual stories about his cow and how he walked her up to the mountain each day to graze. One time he pointed out where he'd gone to school, but it looked like someone's house."

"It probably was. Was it the school or where his teacher lived?" I asked.

"I'm not sure, but your father didn't call him his teacher. He called him *professore*. Said the *professore* wanted him to stay in school past grade four. Said your father was good in math."

"Well, he *was* good in math," I said. "And he taught himself to read and write in English when he came to Canada. I never asked him if he would have liked to stay in school."

Like many who have lost a parent, I wish I had asked him that question and so many more.

I looked around once again. "Where are we?"

"Two minutes from the Kennedy Bar," said Bob.

We stopped at the bar for ice cream because Joe had said, "Figs are ripe. Next time you go to the bar, try the fig ice cream." Joe was sitting at a table in front of the bar playing Scopa with some friends.

"Where you been?" he asked.

"Lunch," said Bob, "We're on our way home."

"Did you go to the restaurant in the woods?"

"I didn't know there was a restaurant there."

"Sure, sure, just past the soccer field," said Joe, turning to his card-playing friends for confirmation. They all nodded.

"There's no sign," I said.

"Sign. Why are you so obsessed with signs, Maria? There is a sign. *'Calcio.'*"

"I meant no sign for the restaurant, unless it's called 'soccer' too."

"No, it's Guerrino alla Selvotta. Guerrino is the man's name — Gary. *Alla* means 'at the,' and Selvotta is the name of the area in Supino where the restaurant's located. They serve good fish. That's their specialty."

The card players were laughing. Was it because I'd expected to see a restaurant sign? Because I thought the restaurant was called Calcio? Or because I believed there was a restaurant in the woods of Supino that specialized in fish?

"Why don't we take you and Angela there for dinner one night, Joe?" offered Bob.

"How about tomorrow?"

"Tomorrow we're going to Alberto's."

"Why you going *there*?"

In bed that night, I said, "Okay, we're having dinner at Alberto's tomorrow night with Franco and Pietro and whoever else is invited. I think you're right. Pietro arranged it because you're all politicians. Or because Alberto's originally from Supino. Maybe Pietro's introducing us to people he thinks we have things in common with. I don't know. But on Wednesday, let's go to Vietri.

"I know you're going to say that we have lots of time, but two weeks can go by quickly. We have to go to my cousin Guido and Liounna's house. I don't want them to feel bad knowing we're in the village and we haven't been to see them. Guido's my oldest cousin in Italy so we really have to get over there soon. And Liounna will want us to come back one day to eat, which is great, but we also have to eat at Joe and Angela's at least once or *they'll* feel bad. We've spent a day with Franco. We're spending another evening at Alberto's, but we have to be careful. Pietro will ask us if we've been here or eaten there, and before we know it, they'll have organized our whole trip. What do you think?"

But when I looked over, Bob was already asleep.

The next day, we did the typical Supino things: cappuccino at the Bar Italia followed by a browse through the street market. We didn't need to buy anything, but the bright umbrellas and the fragrance of peaches and the sound of the tea towels as they flapped in the morning breeze beckoned. Even a small village like Supino has its neighbourhoods, but the outdoor market, in the centre of town, brings everyone together, so we often see women standing chatting near a stall, men sitting and talking at the bar, and children skipping here, kicking a soccer ball there. But when the church bells begin to announce 12 o'clock, the crowd reshuffles. Couples meet up at the street corners, shopping bags are redistributed, and children steal one last kick at the soccer ball before running off to join their families, heading back to their own neighbourhoods. As we climbed the hill back to the *pisciarello*, which is our part of the village, we often walked with a group of neighbours, each one turning off at various laneways or stairways heading home for lunch. *"Buon pranzo,"* we'd wish each other, which means "Have a good lunch."

Pietro said he'd pick us up at seven to drive us to Alberto's house in nearby Frosinone, and the seven o'clock bells were ringing when he knocked at the door. We gathered our things and walked to his car, but he said it was too early to go to Alberto's for the eight o'clock dinner. Bob and I looked at each other, trying to grasp, once again, this Italian concept of time. We'd been ready for seven even though we didn't expect Pietro until closer to eight; then he actually arrived at seven, but here he was telling us we were too early.

"We'll walk down to the bar," Pietro said, and so we did, saying *buona sera* to every villager, at every window and street corner, so that by the time we arrived at the Kennedy Bar, everyone had checked out the style of my dress and the cut of Bob's suit and they knew Pietro was taking us somewhere outside the village. We found Franco at the bar, and we had a drink and discussed whose car we were taking to Enrico's house.

"Wait a minute, wait a minute. Who's Enrico?" I said.

"The mayor," said Pietro.

We took Franco's car to the mayor's house, where we had a tour of his wine cellar and discussed how many bottles of wine to take to Alberto's. No one seemed concerned that it was now past eight. Enrico insisted Bob and I go in his

BMW, so Franco and Pietro followed the mayor's car to Frosinone.

In 30 minutes, we arrived at a beautiful apartment building. The lobby was cool and elegant, with tropical plants and a winding marble staircase. Alberto's wife, Simonetta, stood waiting for us on the second floor and led us straight onto the balcony, where she pointed out Supino, the village's pale lights blinking intermittently on the sloping mountainside.

Alberto soon arrived with a tray of vermouth in thick glasses shaped like gigantic teardrops. After the introductions, with glasses in hand, Alberto proposed a toast: "To Supino!"

Although he was a senator in Rome and lived in the nearby city of Frosinone, Alberto had been born in Supino. He was a gregarious host, leading us to the table, all shiny with silverware, crystal, and candlelight, and as soon as we were seated, he passed the first tray.

"These are polenta squares with different toppings — figs, sausage slices, goat cheese," explained Alberto. "Are you familiar with polenta, Maria?"

I laughed. "Yes, I like it, thank you. We rarely had it at home because my father was convinced it was food for the pigs. Now cornmeal is a delicacy."

"Years ago, my grandfather was the doctor in Supino," said Alberto. "He's dead now, of course, but I'm sure he would have remembered your father."

My father had told me that the doctor owned one of only two cars in the village. The other belonged to the parish priest. "Everyone else walked," my father had said. The doctor also owned some racehorses that he kept at a property up the mountain. "My brother Americo and I used to ride those horses up on the meadow sometimes, even though we weren't supposed to," my father remembered. "They were pretty high-strung, a little jumpy, you know, but we held on. Boy, once they got going, those horses could really run. One time we were racing across the field — Americo was in front, but I was gaining on him — when we saw the doctor's car heading up the road. Americo steered off to some trees. I followed. Americo passed between the trees, and I could still see the horse, but my brother was gone. Then I saw his legs dangling. So I grabbed the tree branch and swung up too."

Partway through the meal, Alberto said, "Tomorrow I'll be at your front door at eight a.m. to take you to Rome for the day. Did Pietro tell you? My wife and I will both come. A little sightseeing. Some shopping. Lunch at a *trattoria* that I know near the Spanish Steps that serves stuffed zucchini blossoms — a Roman delicacy — you'll love them. The Pantheon, of course. The Coliseum, if you like. The Vatican. I'll have you back in Supino by 11 in the evening. Perhaps midnight."

"Thank you," Bob said, and when I nudged him beneath the table, he added, "We can drive down to the coast on Thursday."

"Thursday's the Frosinone market," I said.

"Oh," said Alberto's wife. "Do you like to go to the market? My friend has a nice little stall that sells silk stockings. Would you like me to take you?"

Pietro had said very little throughout the meal but now

he spoke up. "Thursday marks the beginning of the activities for the Feast of the Immigrant, *signora*. City council will want to meet Bob and Maria, our newest residents." He turned to us. "Come around four."

"Where?" asked Bob, but I intervened.

"Pietro, please, I appreciate the invitation, but we're only here for another week and I want to drive down to Vietri sul Mare to buy some tiles for my kitchen."

"Then, of course, you must go," said Pietro. "Why not stay in Italy an extra week or two? I can make a call in the morning to extend your return ticket."

"We can't stay longer. Bob has his coffee business to look after and I'm attending university classes in the fall."

"You need at least a month to relax and enjoy," said Pietro. "I don't think North Americans really understand vacations. Even if you spent a month in Supino, you'd never see everything there is to see and you expect to come and go in a week."

Although I knew Pietro was trying to be helpful by arranging our schedule, I don't think he understood. I was determined to get to Vietri and buy the kitchen tiles.

Before I could respond, Alberto pushed back his chair and said, *"Momento."* He went into the kitchen, returning with the same silver tray that had held the vermouth glasses, only now it held a bottle of liqueur and tiny glasses rimmed in gold. "A toast," he said, as he poured and passed. "To Supino and to Maria's father — son of Supino."

Tears scratched the corners of my eyelids. By the time I'd blinked them back, someone had placed a tray of specialty cheeses from the area, coupled with the first figs of the season and a platter of plums on the damask cloth. Then the aroma of espresso wafted out from the kitchen door, so Pietro and Bob were discussing a tour of the coffee roasting plant in Frosinone on Friday.

The next day over a bottle of wine in Joe's backyard, I explained how I wanted to drive down the coast and everyone else in Supino had other plans for us.

"You don't like these people?" asked Joe sympathetically.

"No, no, they're very nice."

"You didn't want to visit Rome?"

"Yes, but I had planned —"

"You come to Supino to be in your father's village and then you don't want to be here. This makes no sense, Maria. And you worry too much about everything. Where's Bob? It's almost time for supper and Angela is making *pasta e fagioli*. That's pasta and beans — a Supinese specialty."

"Yes, I know, Joe, but we can't spend all our time in Supino just going from one house to another to eat. Soon our holiday will be over and we won't have actually done anything."

"That's no problem, Maria. You just stay longer."

Three

Back in Toronto, we were instantly immersed in our big-city life. I balanced my family with finishing my BA at York University, while Bob juggled the family, the coffee company, his councillor role at City Hall, and a lot of committee meetings, including the Supino Social Club. Bob was seldom home in the evenings and busy most weekends: he didn't see as much of the family as he would have liked. He solved that by involving us in the organization's activities. We decorated a float for the Weston Santa Claus parade; we enlisted our oldest nephew Rick to drive the truck and our older children to walk alongside handing out candy canes; we put younger relatives in costumes, and they sat on the back of the flatbed truck and waved red-mittened hands at the crowd. At the opening of the Weston Farmers' Market and at other community events, we helped to set up or take down tables and displays, and we worked behind those tables selling cupcakes, operating the face-painting stand, or pushing raffle tickets. When we finished participating in one event, the planning would start for the next.

Even our backyard was a beehive of activity as Bob and his friends built contraptions for the opening-day festivities for the Weston Farmers' Market: a water-dunking tank, cardboard outhouses on wheels for the outhouse race, and beds on wheels for the bed race. When the yard wasn't filled with construction projects, it was filled with people, because Bob had hosted a fundraising barbecue for the seniors and it had been so successful he expanded it to include other groups. The kids and I were often barbecuing Italian sausages, serving drinks, and cleaning up afterwards.

And then there were the family celebrations: birthdays, holidays, graduations, showers, weddings, corn roasts, and Sunday dinners. Bob had grown up without this constant celebration of . . . everything . . . but he thought it was wonderful to gather on some cousin's property with a bonfire, bushels of corn and pots of boiling water, guitars and harmonicas, and pizza — always pizza.

So our days in Toronto were full, but by January's end we were already starting to look forward to the peacefulness of the village.

The following spring, as we were planning our trip to Supino, Bob said, "I'd like to spend a few days in Venice while we're in Italy."

"How are you going to get a trip to Venice past the villagers' plans?" I asked.

"We call Joe as usual to ask him to get the house ready. We

visit Venice first, and then we drive to Supino and pretend we've just come from the airport. Or we leave Supino early, drive up to Venice for a few days, and fly home from there. They'll never know."

"We better go to Venice first," I said. "Or I'll spend all my time in Supino trying not to mention Venice. I can just hear Joe: 'Venice? Why you want to go there? Costs a lotta money and there's nothing but tourists and water, and the water don't smell so good.'"

So we booked a flight to Venice and on a warm spring morning in May, after a delayed take-off, we were finally approaching the Venice airport. There was a problem on the runway and we had to circle the airport for over an hour before receiving permission to land. Then our luggage was delayed. After that, the bus that goes to central Venice was late and, finally, toward five o'clock, hot, hungry, and cranky, we were squashed onto the blue bus with other equally grumpy travellers.

The young woman sitting in front of us turned to her companion and asked, "Will the hotel hold our reservation no matter what time we arrive?"

"Absolutely," replied her seatmate.

"Thank goodness. I'd hate to have to start looking for a hotel this late in the day."

"Only a fool would come to Venice without a reservation," assured the know-it-all.

I took an immediate dislike to that woman. Bob and I were the fools that had come to Venice without a hotel reservation. Bob squeezed my hand and used Joe's favourite expression: "Don't worry about it."

By six o'clock we were in Central Venice, lined up at a ticket booth trying to figure out how much the boat fare cost. As soon as the *vaporetto* arrived, we were swept on board among students and knapsacks, tourists and luggage, elegant Venetians carrying equally elegant dogs, and bored businessmen with their noses in the news. I kept one eye on the luggage and the other on Bob, who got seasick easily. Whenever we pulled up to a *vaporetto* stop, I'd raise my eyebrows: *This one?*

Not yet, he'd signal, and we'd keep going. I knew he was watching for a residential area.

By the time we reached St. Mark's Square, there were only tourists left on our *vaporetto* and more waiting on the platform ready to board. We started back toward the piazza where we'd begun and got off at the first stop, Accademia. Right beside the boat stop was an outdoor pizza restaurant with the prices posted on a menu out front.

"*Troppo,*" declared Bob, another expression he'd learned from Joe. It meant "too much." We walked away from the canal and the crowds, and as the sun was beginning to set, we found a small café and ordered two espressos. The bartender slid them across the counter without a glance, continuing his conversation with the locals leaning against the bar. The coffee was awfully strong.

"*Scusa,*" I said, "*zucchero?*" and the bartender flicked me a sugar packet.

"Is there a hotel near here?" Bob asked.

The barman pointed vaguely toward the open door and the setting sun.

"If we were in Supino . . ." I said to Bob, picking up my suitcase.

"I know. He'd walk us right to the hotel."

"And haggle for the best price for the room."

"And buy us a drink before he left."

"Of course, we'd probably have to go to his house for lunch the next day."

"Meet some neighbour who'd been to Toronto 20 years earlier and —"

"We're just tired. I'm sure once we get a good night's sleep, Venice will charm us in the morning."

We trudged from one full hotel to another until we decided it would be more sensible for me to sit on the bench with the luggage while Bob scouted out a vacancy. It was pitch dark before he returned. "Found a room," he said. He passed me a thin slice of cold pizza. "Don't even ask me how much I had to pay for that." And we were off.

The sign out front said, "American Hotel," and underneath in smaller letters, "Air-conditioned." The lobby was lovely and cool. Our room, which the owner had assured Bob was the last vacant room in Venice, was in the attic. It had whitewashed walls, slanted ceilings, and no air conditioning. We fell onto the bed and sweated until dawn.

The next morning, we found a more European-style *pensione* where our meals were included in the price. Bob said, "If Joe heard how much this place charges, he'd turn our Supino house into a permanent *pensione*."

"You know, Joe and Angela are celebrating their 25th wedding anniversary this year," I said. "I thought I'd keep my eye out for something special. Maybe a liqueur set or a hand-blown glass vase. What do you think?"

"I think you're going to have a hard time explaining how

you bought a gift made in Venice, without admitting that we were here."

"Joe's pretty agreeable if we bring a gift for Angela or Marco. He doesn't grill us on the price or say, 'What you bring this for?'"

In a tiny shop, we found a beautiful wine decanter and six glasses, all hand-blown in the colours of a Venetian sunset. Bob did not say *"Troppo"* when I showed him the price, even though we both knew it was.

On our last evening, we found a gondolier half-asleep in his gondola parked in a small canal. "Come back in half an hour," he suggested, tipping his straw hat over his eyes, so we had a glass of *prosecco* at a nearby bar and then returned. At first, we were part of a flotilla of gondolas out on the grand canal, with several gondoliers serenading the tourists with *"O Sole Mio"* as the cameras clicked and whirred, but, as the sun began its descent, our gondolier steered us into a smaller canal, and another and another, so that by the time the sun had set, we were in the dark heart of a Venice so silent we could hear the touch of the gondolier's oar on the still water and the drizzle of the water as it dripped back into the canal.

In the morning we left Venice, picked up our rental car in the piazza, and drove south to Supino. As we returned home to the village, we were as carefree as a couple of teenagers, racing down the *autostrada* with the windows wide open and our secret side trip to Venice safely behind us. We stopped at the bar without a name just before the Quattro Strade.

"Hey," said the bartender, "I know you. *Espresso senza zucchero*, right?"

"*Sì,*" said Bob, apparently one of the few visitors to the bar who ordered his coffee *senza zucchero* — without sugar.

"I thought so," added the bartender. "The Summer Supinese. Welcome back." He slid a saucer full of biscotti down the counter. "My wife made these."

"We'll be home in half an hour," said Bob as we pulled out of the parking lot half an hour later, but we were stopped by a flock of sheep changing pastures. The shepherd tipped his hat to us when the last straggler was in the field, and we began the ascent into Supino. We passed the Kennedy Bar and stopped at the red light on the hill. A wide plastic ribbon was strung across the street. On a small piece of paper, stapled to the ribbon, was an *X*.

Bob made a U-turn back to the Kennedy Bar, a left onto *via case nuove*, the street of new houses, and around behind the Bar Italia. At *via d'Italia*, there was another ribbon and another slip of paper waving at us. Bob made a second U-turn and we headed up the mountain to the unnamed street that connects the mountain road to the water fountain at the top of *via condotto vecchio*. The road was open, but no one was filling water jugs. We parked on the street across from our house and began unloading the car.

"*Finalmente,*" Angela called out the window. "Leave that stuff in the house. Hurry up. The *festa* . . ." The six o'clock church bells blocked the rest of the sentence. ". . . And, Maria, don't forget to take your sweater."

No one ever told us the locations of the *festas*. We simply followed the villagers down the street. As Joe said, "Everyone goes." Today we walked toward the centre of the village and waited at the traffic light. There was a large red plastic ribbon tied around the light and a small white paper that said, *"Mostra dell'Azalea."* My father had told me that the azalea flower grows particularly well in Supino — something about the minerals in the soil, the elevation of the village, and the rainfall — so the villagers hold a festival every spring to celebrate. Someone beeped and we stepped aside: a city truck rumbled past, five or six azalea plants in large tin tubs rattling in the open back.

"Those plants come from near the *quattro strade*," said the flower-shop man. "People who live there can winter the azalea in their sheds. That's the problem. Town people don't have enough space. They have to keep pruning. Keep the plants small. The outsiders transplant to larger pots and the azaleas grow as big as bushes. People who live outside of town — what do you call that? The suburbs? If you live in the suburbs of Supino, you have the advantage when it comes to size."

"Is there a prize for the biggest azalea?" I asked.

"Prize? It's not a contest. It's a show. You know, like you have in Canada, a flower show."

The light changed and we carried on, past the butcher, the baker, and up to the piazza across from the Church of Santa Maria Maggiore. Here, at the top of the hill, was an intersection of three streets and a policewoman. She was allowing cars to travel down the hill to the Kennedy Bar, and beyond to the *quattro strade*, but she wasn't permitting the cars to turn into the village *centro*. The policewoman was arguing that point with a man with a red face and a blue Fiat.

The third street leads past the statue that honours sol-
diers killed in the two world wars, then past the barber, the
shop that sells men's shirts, the stone steps that guide you
to the oldest part of the village, the store that sells postcards
but not stamps, the City Hall, and up to the third piazza at
the Church of San Pietro. The street was overflowing with
azaleas in every shade, from palest pink to red-hot fuchsia,
crammed into metal washtubs, terra cotta planters, cement
pots, tins, and plastic pails. Every size from a two-litre olive-
oil tin to a square-metre washtub was represented. And the
villagers, dressed in their Sunday best, paraded among the
plants, admiring and comparing.

Bob took a few photos from the bottom of the street,
trying to capture the abundance of plants and people. "It's
no use," he said. "You can't really catch it in a four-by-six."

We wove our way to the top of the hill, where Joe was
helping to set up tables in front of the church.

"What are the tables for?" asked Bob.

Joe made that slight circular motion with his hand.
"Pizza," he said. "*Vino, taralli* cookies, and *ginettes* . . . Luigi —
he lives over there — we put the beer table in his cantina to
keep it cool. The peanut roaster comes. We put a few chairs
for the old people. You have this in Toronto, no?"

"We have a spring garden show," I began, "but it's indoors."

"Sure, sure. Too cold to have it on the street."

But it was so much more than the weather that made the
difference. Here in Supino, there were no posters advertising the flower show, because everyone knew it was held on
the first Sunday in May, and people of all ages came out to

celebrate the azalea flowers in bloom. It was a simple thing to close off the main street every spring with a red plastic ribbon and a hand-printed sign with the letter *X*. Several artists had set up among the plants with easels or sketchpads, a tray of watercolours or charcoals. There were no vendor permits, special liquor licenses, or food inspectors in sight. Elisabetta, who was confined to a wheelchair in an apartment on the square, could lower a basket packed with squares of thick pizza wrapped in waxed paper. Anyone could take a piece and call up, *"Buona, Elisabetta,"* knowing that Elisabetta's pizza was thick with sweet tomato sauce and topped with a basil leaf from her balcony garden. People put a euro or two in the empty basket before she hoisted it back up.

All the houses and apartments that overlooked the square had azalea plants on their windowsills or doorsteps, and someone had even placed a small red azalea on the window-sill of a deserted house. City trucks drove to the outskirts of Supino to pick up the plants for the show. Local villagers carried their own flowers to the street and brought the larger pots by wheelbarrow. Later the Supino band would play its usual repertoire of songs, and couples would dance on the cobblestones. There'd be fireworks set off behind the church and visible from everywhere in the village. Bob and I would walk home, hand in hand, on cobblestone streets lit by Supino stars. Angela would call *"Buonanotte!"* from her kitchen window.

In our back bedroom, which overlooked the ravine and the mountain, we'd lift our bed carefully and tiptoe it across the room. Even though Angela had warned us that the night air was damp and we shouldn't sleep beneath the open window, we pushed the shutters wide to the night sky. In the morning, we'd return the bed to its assigned place, but tonight, we'd sleep beneath the light of the Big and Little Dipper framed in our window.

Our youngest daughter, Kathryn, usually accompanied us on our annual trips back to the village, but this year she'd stayed in Toronto to write her grade II exams, and now we drove into Rome to pick her up at the airport. As soon as we returned to the village, Kathryn reconnected with a group of Supinese teenagers. She soon knew about all the markets in the villages that surrounded Supino: Saturday for Ferentino, Thursday for Frosinone, a different day for both of the neighbouring hilltop villages of Patrica and Morolo, and some days a market on the road that leads to Terracina and the beach. That market featured beach essentials like towels, umbrellas, plastic pails and shovels, sunblock, various fresh fruit, sandals, bottled water, bikinis, and, by mid-July, watermelon.

In the village, the teenagers took over the water fountain area in the evenings, listening to music and talking. Villagers would come to fill their water jugs and grandmothers hung out of kitchen windows that overlooked the street and the fountain piazza, so the teenagers, like everyone else, were always under someone's gaze. During the summer, rock bands or Italian pop singers performed at one of the piazzas for the teenagers; other nights, some of the young people played in their own bands at restaurants and bars in the area.

One afternoon we were sitting on our front steps, Bob and I watching the pedestrians go by, Kathryn sketching the pale blue chicory flower growing in a tin can on the windowsill of a deserted house across the street.

"Davide's band is playing in Ferentino tonight," she said. "Is it okay if I go?"

Davide was the son of our next-door neighbour Peppe. On the day that Kathryn arrived in the village, Peppe had asked Davide to show her around and Davide had pulled up on his motorcycle, passed Kathryn a spare helmet, and they'd roared off. He'd given Kathryn the little tour of Supino on the first day of her arrival and he'd come by every day since. Kathryn had loaned him some CDs; he brought his artwork over to show her; they discussed books he'd read in his English literature class at Rome University. They were both interested in photography and the same kind of music.

"How are you getting to Ferentino?" I said. The town was half an hour away.

"A few cars . . . you know," said Kathryn, and she used the circular hand motion so common in the village.

"What time does the band play? What time will you get back?"

"She'll be fine," said Bob. "Everyone's always watching anyway."

"Here in Supino they're watching. I don't know about Ferentino."

"Don't worry, Maria," called Angela from her kitchen window. "My girl's going. Marco too. It's okay, Caterina can go."

Bob made the circular hand motion. "You know what?"

he said. "I'll take you somewhere different for dinner tonight. We'll go to the restaurant in the woods."

"I don't know if it even exists, Bob. It might be a joke. Think about it — seafood in the woods?"

"Angela," called Bob. "Have you ever eaten at the seafood restaurant in the woods?"

"Restaurant?" repeated Angela, as if the very word was foreign.

That night at eight, instead of heading off to our usual places, the dining room at the Hotel Dalma or the restaurant at the Pensione Bompiani, we drove to the Kennedy Bar, past the hardware store, and to the second street where the blue sign, "*Calcio,*" was nailed onto a fence post. As soon as we turned onto that street, if indeed a path can be called a street, the roadway was pitch dark. The only light came when we passed a driveway where a small box was cemented to a pillar that supported a wrought-iron gate. In the small box, a dim light bulb illuminated the owner's name.

"This can't be the right road," I said, but Bob assured me, "Joe said the restaurant's past the soccer field and we haven't passed the soccer field yet."

We heard the sounds of soccer fans before we saw the floodlights. There were more lights on that field than on the entire *via condotto vecchio*. But as soon as we passed the field, we were back in the darkness.

"Does this road actually go anywhere or do we have to turn around to get back to town?" I asked.

"I think it connects to the street where Joe said the organic farmers live — look."

Two small lights illuminated the box mounted on the stone

pillars, showing the owner's name: *"Guerrino alla Selvotta."* Bob stopped and rolled down his window: the chirping of crickets, the crunch of gravel, and the slam of a car door. From deep in the woods came the scent of burning wood and the clatter of dishes and silverware. Bob backed up and swung into the gravel parking lot. There were a few other cars, but no lights of course. The sky was littered with stars. Hand in hand we walked across the gravel and up the stone steps to an outdoor patio where dozens of slender beech trees shared space with planters of geraniums and trailing ivy and a dozen tables and chairs. Customers sitting at half the tables: no waiter in sight.

We walked into the restaurant, where a woman was rolling out balls of dough on a floured counter and, behind her, a young man was pulling a bubbling pizza from the oven. He slid the pizza onto a plate and called, "Luigi." A moustached waiter grabbed the plate and was gone as quickly as he appeared.

"Too crowded in here," said Bob, and we returned to the quiet of the terrace, choosing a table near the window so the light from the restaurant shone on the white linen. "Just in case there's a menu," he said. "We'll be able to read it."

"I've never seen a menu in Supino, unless you count that chalkboard listing the specials at the Bompiani."

"You mean the specials that you try to order and the waiter wags his finger at you?"

"Exactly."

"Joe said a menu's a North American idea," said Bob. "It makes no sense. Nobody who lives in Supino needs a menu to tell them what's growing in the garden. If the artichokes are ready or the peaches are ripe, that's what you're going to get in the restaurant. Why waste money on a menu?"

A young boy, no more than 12, wearing the waiter's uniform of black trousers and immaculate white shirt, placed a bottle of water on our table. *"Acqua frizzante?"* he asked, and was gone before we could answer. Bob poured the bubbly water and I watched a waiter balance a gigantic tray through the door and onto a serving table set up nearby. The young boy took plates of seafood antipasto to one table, dishes of spaghetti with clams to a second, and plates of grilled trout to a third. Bob didn't eat fish.

"What are you going to order?" I asked.

"I memorized it from the phrase book," he said. *"Senza pesce.* Without fish."

The young boy was back. *"Vino?"* he asked as he placed a bottle of white on the table and pulled the cork. *"Pane?"* he added, putting the breadbasket on our table. The boy put a cruet of dark green olive oil in front of Bob and made the circular hand motion between the bread and the oil. *"Buon appetito,"* he said.

The waiter soon arrived without a menu. Instead, he offered two plates with tiny shrimps, scallops, and calamari all heaped on a bed of arugula.

"Senza pesce," said Bob, using the finger wag.

"Senza pesce?" repeated the waiter.

"Sì, senza pesce," repeated Bob.

A shrug from the waiter before he carried Bob's plate back inside, calling out to the kitchen, *"Senza pesce."* Two minutes later he was back with a new plate: cheese, salami and some other cured meats, olives, pickled vegetables, and a lone clamshell holding a quartered lemon. *"Signor,"* the young waiter instructed, *"antipasto della montagna."*

"Appetizers of the mountain," I translated.

Two businessmen sat down at the table beside us. One waved down the waiter and ordered *Asti Spumante*. They lit up cigars. The young boy arrived with an ice bucket and the waiter twirled the champagne bottle before wrapping it in a cloth. *"Attenzione,"* he called just before he popped the cork. Those few seconds of silence while we waited for the explosive sound were followed by the loud voices of the two men. Between the scent of their cigars and the sound of their excited talk, the night took on a more hectic feel.

Bob put his hand on mine. "If you listen carefully, you can hear the crickets chirping."

Beside us, one man checked his watch, drained his glass, and scraped his chair back. The other peeled off a few bills and called to the boy. A quick glance at Bob's hand on mine, a quick conversation, and the men were gone. The boy brought the champagne bottle to our table. "From the *signore*."

We drank leftover champagne from Supinese strangers; the waiter brought us linguine with tomato sauce. He followed that with a barbecued trout for me, and a *spiedini* for Bob. When Bob inspected the barbecued meat on the wooden stick, the waiter immediately reassured, *"Senza pesce."* Tossed salad arrived without us ordering it. We finished off the champagne. The waiter decided to top off our meal with a dessert of cooked cream covered with wild berries.

"S*ignor Bob*?" asked a man. "I am Guerrino. Call me Gary. You must be Mrs. Bob. Sorry to hear about your father. My family didn't know him. He was a mountain man and we are of the woods. How do you like my little place?"

"One of the prettiest restaurants I've ever seen," said Bob. "And my business takes me into a lot of restaurants."

"I heard. You are the coffee man. How you like our Italian coffee?" he asked.

"Better than ours."

"So," Gary said, as he pulled out a chair. "May I? Your meal okay?"

"Molto buono," said Bob.

"I have relatives in Toronto. I go every winter for a few months. They take me around to some places to try North American food. My cousin took me to a Toronto restaurant made to look like the inside of a ship — maybe you know it. I ordered a grilled trout. The waiter, he brings the fish on a plate and puts it in front of me. He doesn't cut off the head. He doesn't cut off the tail. He doesn't take out the skeleton. He just leaves the knife for me to debone my own fish. Like I work for him. Did you have the trout?"

"I did," I replied. "It was delicious, but Bob doesn't eat fish."

"I see. Come back tomorrow. I make you something special. Ey, Maurizio," he called to the boy, followed by a string of quick Italian. In a few minutes, the boy was back with a silver tray holding a sweating bottle of *limoncello* and three frosty glasses. "I make a toast," he said. "To your father."

In a darkened corner, an old man wearing a fedora opened up his accordion case. The accordion exhaled its preliminary sigh and the man began to play. I'd never heard the tune before. People leaned back in their chairs, heads dipped onto others' shoulders, the waiter tucked his silver tray beneath his elbow and leaned on the doorway, and the woman paused from rolling her pizza dough. Stars poked through the dark Supino night sky, blinking here and there as if they recognized the haunting tune from decades past.

"I love it here," said Bob. I wasn't sure if he meant the restaurant or the village. "I've been thinking Joe's right. We should spend more time in Supino."

"Don't you think you'd get a little restless after a couple of weeks?"

"I've been thinking I could do something while we're here. If we stayed for the summer, Joe said Bianca could use some help in the mornings at the Bar Italia. Her husband got a job driving the delivery truck for Lavazza, so he won't be around in the day, and their son's too young to be much help yet."

"What about when summer's over?"

"Joe says summer's the busiest time for a bar in Supino. You know, the immigrants who come back to the village to visit their relatives and the people from Rome who have summer places here. In the winter, business is slower. It's the opposite of the coffee business in Toronto, where our customers are busier in the winter months and things slow down in the summer."

"I don't know, Bob, it wouldn't be much of a vacation if you spent your time working."

"It would just be in the morning for a couple of hours. I like to get up early anyway, and making coffee and cappuccino isn't really work. Plus I like to talk to people. It's just a thought — something to consider."

"You don't really speak Italian."

"I could pick up the words I need easily enough."

"You're used to running your own business. Would you be okay to work for someone else?"

"If I wasn't, I could always buy a place and open my own bar."

I laughed. I thought he was kidding.

Four

On the days after the azalea show, routine returned to *via condotto vecchio*. Every morning, we'd wander down to the shops to buy our day's supply of fruit, vegetables, and bread, and each day, our list of groceries grew shorter. No need to buy eggs when Joe left warm ones in a basket on our doorstep every morning. No need to buy fresh figs or plums or strawberries from the greengrocer because the neighbours brought them to the house by the basketful. No need to buy sausages because Alfredo, who lives around the corner and often joined us at the bar for our morning coffee, brought us jars of sausages preserved in olive oil. We could not reciprocate with fruits or vegetables because we had nothing growing in our tiny backyard except the plants that Joe's brother Benito planted there.

In the afternoons, it was very hot in our backyard. Good for Benito's plants, but not so good for us. I thought that if we could plant a shade tree or construct an awning, it would provide relief from the sun and we'd be able to use the patio in the afternoons. I mentioned this to Joe.

"Sure, sure," he said. "I'll plant a grapevine. Grows very fast. Makes good shade."

The next day there was a cutting sitting on our cracked terrazzo patio. My cousin Guido saw it when he stopped by. Guido had spent a few years in Toronto in the '50s before returning to Italy, where he and Liounna live in Rome during the winter but spend the summers in Supino. They have a little house on a small patch of land across the ravine. Guido brought some asparagus and leaf lettuce from his garden.

As soon as we stepped onto the patio, Guido reached into his pocket for his penknife and sliced a fading rose from one of Benito's rose bushes. "You have to prune these," he said.

"They're not my roses," I explained. "Benito takes care of the garden."

"Did you buy this?" asked Guido, fingering the grape cutting.

"No, no," I reassured him, "Joe brought it over to plant."

"If you allow your neighbour to plant on your land, the harvest belongs to the neighbour."

"The grapevine's not for growing grapes," I tried to explain. "It's for shade. You see how sunny it is out here at this time of day."

"So I'll bring you a cutting from my grapevine and you'll be able to keep the grapes."

"I just want the shade."

"What's the matter with you, Maria? You can't eat shade."

I watched Guido walk from the back door of our house across the five metres to our front door, where he stopped and rummaged around in the tiny closet under the stairs. I raised my eyebrows at Bob; he turned up the palms of his hands.

A few moments later, Guido returned with the beach umbrella Kathryn had bought at the market. The opened umbrella provided a small circle of shade. "Hold this," he told Bob, as he pulled some twine from his pocket and tied the umbrella handle to the two-by-four post that marked the edge of our patio. "Next time, I'll bring some nails." Then, without warning, Guido picked up Joe's grapevine and tossed it into the ravine. "See you on Sunday," he said, putting on his cap and heading for the door.

It wasn't long before we had to explain the missing grapevine. The following morning, we heard several sharp whistles in our backyard that could only have come from Joe's brother, Benito, who is deaf and communicates with hand gestures and whistles. Two minutes later, both Benito and Joe were in our yard.

"Okay, okay," we heard Joe say. I could imagine Joe patting Benito's arm to calm him. "Bob," he called up to the open bedroom window.

Bob put his finger to his lips as we carefully lifted our bed from beneath the window and tiptoed it back to where Angela wanted us to keep it. "What should we say?" I whispered as we climbed down the stairs.

Bob turned up the palms of his hands. "Guido was just trying to help," said Bob as soon as we got to the backyard. "He tied this umbrella here to give some shade."

"Benito says someone pruned the rose bush."

"Guido didn't know it was Benito's job," I said.

"What the bloody hell is going on?" said Joe. "A man comes into someone else's yard, Maria, and prunes his roses and throws his plants away and sticks up an umbrella that can only make shade for one person when a grapevine could shade the whole place." Joe made an expansive sweep of his arm across our ten-foot-by-ten-foot patio. "Why you stick up for him?"

"He's my cousin."

"I forgot." Joe made a motion to Benito, who responded with a series of gestures. "Benito says forget the grapevine. Since you want shade, he'll make you something special with pipes and plastic sheets. He just needs some time to find everything." Joe reached into his pocket for his penknife and approached the umbrella.

"Let's leave the umbrella here," suggested Bob. "It'll make some shade in the meantime."

"In the meantime," Joe said, "you come to my house in the afternoon. It's shady in my backyard."

The next morning we woke to the rumble of a truck on *via condotto vecchio*, accompanied by loud voices. We stood on our balcony and watched the city workers put up the wooden arches with lights that marked every *festa*. Two street sweepers working in unison to brush the cobblestones followed the city workers down the street. Usually Benito swept our street each morning, but today he stood in the doorway of Joe's house, leaning on his own broom and watching. A small crew of painters, dressed in white jackets and hats, carrying buckets and brushes and long-handled rollers, followed the street sweepers.

"It's like a parade of workers," I said to Bob. "And it's not even eight o'clock yet."

The painters stopped and pulled out cigarettes and matches. The scent of tobacco joined the scent of coffee wafting from Angela's kitchen window. Joe's garage door opened, but when Joe saw the painters, he left the door open and came out to the street. He pointed to Benito's broom and the street sweepers, joking that Benito was out of a job. Benito gave Joe a punch on the arm.

In a few minutes, the street sweepers had reached the bottom of our street where it intersects with the road that goes up to Santa Nicola and the street that goes down to the Bar Italia. There's a *piazzetta*, a little piazza, at that intersection in front of the water fountain that doesn't work. Benito and the painters moved down to the *piazzetta*, and Benito sat on the bench to watch while the painters marked off five parking spots with white paint. Joe jumped in his car and swung left, heading up the hill away from the village.

"All the roads closed today," he called up to us. "San Cataldo."

My father had told me a few things about the Feast of San Cataldo. Schools were closed but the stores stayed open with extra stock for the *festa*. He said that people came from other villages to take part in the May 10th celebration. The day began with a sunrise Mass, and families arrived the night before, sleeping in the fields outside of Supino in order to be at the church on time. After the Mass, a group of red-robed men, including my grandfather, carried the statue of San Cataldo on a platform out to the piazza where the saint would spend the day in the spring sunshine and people would come to kiss his plaster feet and ask for favours or give thanks for favours granted. Dad was a little vague on the religious aspect of the feast, because for him it was more about the school holiday and the special foods his mother made for that day, as well as the fireworks at night. Dad said a few vendors set up tables on the main street selling things you couldn't buy in the village: *prosciutto* cutters, goldfish swimming in bowls, budgies in bamboo cages, factory-made garden tools, copper pots, and, sometimes, if the travelling street vendors had reached Supino, exotic trinkets from Ethiopia. One year, my father said, there was even a fire-eater.

For the rest of the day, wherever we walked, we passed workers cleaning and decorating the village. In the shops, the owners were busy stocking shelves and washing windows. At the store beside the jewellery shop, the owner hung skeins of brightly coloured embroidery threads in her front window and built pyramids with balls of wool. Inside, the butcher prepared a few dozen freshly plucked chickens for the grill outside. The baker set up extra bread racks to hold the extra loaves. The shoe-store ladies put three tables in front of their store with an assortment of shoes that had been in style 20 years earlier and a sign that read, *"Speciale."* In the window of the postcard store, the woman removed her usual display of black-and-white postcards from the '50s with their pinked edges and faded images, and replaced them with a stack of small white paper bags, a silver scoop, a scale, and an assortment of jars filled with penny candies.

Outside the store window, a collection of children pointed excitedly at licorice cigars and sour keys and jawbreakers and lemon slices and red cinnamon lips and little waxy candies that looked like Coke bottles. Except for the hazelnut nougat and almond torrone that their parents made at Christmas time, candy was a rarity in the village. The only thing the shopkeepers didn't have that day was time to chat. A quick *"Buongiorno"* was all we got as we passed.

On the morning of the 10th, when we left the house as usual to head to Bar Italia, Bob had barely closed the front door before Angela called out her window, "Make sure you put all the locks."

On our street, we'd grown accustomed to the sounds of our neighbours' doors. Joe's garage opened with a whir; next door, Peppe's opened in tinny increments, usually followed by the roar of Davide's motorcycle. We recognized the sound of Sam's truck and the distressed vehicles making their way up to Carlo the mechanic's shop. In the same way, we knew the click of everyone's front door, the swish of their window shutters, and even the sound of their friends' voices as they stood on the street calling up to an open window. And our neighbours knew the metallic click of our front door key, the small scratch of the balcony shutter as it scraped on the marble floor when Kathryn opened it each morning, the purring engine of our rental car, and even the tap of our footsteps as we ran up and down the steps of number 10. Our front door locked automatically but you could add the deadlock with two twists of the key. We never bothered, but today we obeyed Angela's instructions.

A lot of unfamiliar cars were parked all along the street.

We'd never been in the village for the annual San Cataldo feast and had no idea of the crowds that would arrive that day. There were so many people in the Bar Italia that Joe was helping behind the counter. As soon as he saw us, he motioned us outside and joined us in a couple of minutes with two espressos on a tray.

"We usually have cappuccino in the morning," I said.

"No time for cappuccino today. Bob, you have any money?" At Bob's nod, Joe continued, "Keep it in your pocket. Just bring out what you need. Small bills. Don't let anyone see a roll. Count your change. Ask how much before you buy. Don't pay what they ask. If they say, '*Americano?*' you say, '*No. Sono Supinese.*' Don't speak English. Maria, you have any money?"

"No."

"That's good."

Joe put our empty cups on the tray and went back inside. As soon as we rounded the curve, where the shoe store sits in the middle of the street, everything became clear. The street was closed to traffic — we could not even see the traffic light for striped awnings and colourful canopies covering tables and carts of every size and featuring every possible item one could imagine. Cylindrical candles with images of Jesus or Mary or San Cataldo stood beside helium balloons featuring SpongeBob and Garfield. There were barrels of olives and tables of dried *baccalà* and baskets of lemons and *taralli* cookies threaded on wooden dowels and embroidered pillowcases and shovels and espresso cups and wicker baskets, and ladies' underwear hanging everywhere.

We had to elbow our way through the tunnel. The

bakery, where we often bought a couple of slices of pizza, had a lineup stretching beyond the flower shop. Across the street the butcher was cooking sausages on one barbecue and *spiedini* on another; the barber from next door worked alongside the butcher cutting open the buns. A stranger, with a pushcart full of religious candles, stood on the other side of the butcher.

"Butcher, baker, candlestick maker," Bob said to me.

The candle seller turned immediately. *"Americano?"* he asked, trying to put a candle in Bob's hand. "Good price. Only five euro."

We shook our heads and kept walking. By the time we reached the top of the hill, where the three streets intersected, we'd been offered good prices on many things we didn't want. As we looked down to the Kennedy Bar, all we could see was our main street stuffed with people, our sidewalks stuffed with vendors. Beside us the piazza was filled with an art display of velvet paintings depicting Mary, Joseph, or Elvis.

We slipped inside the Church of Santa Maria Maggiore, but even here, an African vendor displayed his carved wooden animals on a cloth spread in front of the Holy Water font. A small boy stood guard by the front door, watching for the priest or police. A soft whistle and the vendor would fold the four corners of his cloth and they'd be out the side door. We sidestepped the vendor and went back outside, moving away from the crowd until we could go no further. Our backs pressed against the post office, which was closed of course, we watched the turbulent sea of strangers. Above the crowd, a pile of wicker baskets bobbed along. The baskets were followed by a bunch of whirring pinwheels and a long bamboo pole stacked with *ginette* cookies, Supino's version of that North American invention, the doughnut.

Some commotion erupted around the baskets, and the crowd pulled back a little to reveal a small man wearing a coolie hat and wheeling a pushcart loaded sky-high with baskets of every size and description. He was arguing with a woman who had set up a display of tablecloths, tea towels, and handkerchiefs all hung helter-skelter on a portable clothesline. Two clothespins held a sign announcing "100% *cottone*" but no price. The voices grew louder. The man waved a paper at the woman.

"Is that a parking ticket?" I asked Bob, but before he could answer, I heard three sharp blasts from the policewoman's whistle. One of the strangers in the crowd responded with a wolf whistle and that started another commotion. Before the policewoman could ask what the problem was, the man showed her his paper and pointed to the building. The woman said, "*Casa mia. Casa mia.*"

"I think she lives in that house," said Bob. "She's married to the street cleaner."

"No," said someone from the crowd. "To the postman."

"Who's the man with the baskets?"

"A foreigner. From Morolo."

Morolo was the village half a day's walk away from Supino.

"I think I've seen that man before," I said to Bob.

"Sure," replied someone. "He sells at the Tuesday market."

Now I remembered him. We'd even bought a large and rather expensive hand-woven wicker basket from him to store

our firewood and he'd tossed in a complimentary breadbasket. Joe had been a little upset with us for spending the
money when he had already given us a wooden crate that had
once held grapes. We'd pointed out that the large basket was
handmade, and showed him the breadbasket we'd received
— "for free." Joe showed us the faded stamp almost hidden
on the bottom of the basket that read "Made in China." A
few spectators were now browsing the man's baskets and the
woman's cloths. Cristina, from the *tabacchi* store, held up an
embroidered tea towel and asked the price. The two women
haggled. The man began unloading his baskets.

"*No, no,*" said the woman. "*Casa mia.*"

"*Un permesso,*" replied the man.

"*Quattro euro?*" repeated Cristina, fingering the cloth.
"*Troppo.*"

"*Un momento, un momento,*" said the policewoman. She spoke
directly to the woman: "This man has a permit issued by the
city for *via Regina Margherita* 13 and *numero* 13 is painted right
here on the street."

"*Casa mia.*"

"Yes, it's your house, *signora,* but today and tomorrow he
has *un permesso* to use this space. Just for the *festa.*"

"I'm selling my cloths here."

"Do you have *un permesso, signora?*"

"I don't need. This is my house."

Cristina offered the woman three euros, instead of four,
for the tea towel. "She has the right to sell in front of her
own house," she said.

The street sweeper said, "The street belongs to the village. I sweep it every day."

"I sweep," said the woman.

"My job."

"If you did a good job I wouldn't have to."

"She doesn't have un permesso," said a stranger.

"A number painted on the street," said Cristina, "means nothing."

"It means the man can sell his baskets there for two days," said the policewoman.

"He's not even from our village."

"That doesn't matter. He has the permesso and she doesn't."

"She lives here."

The debate roared around us, like the rounds of a campfire song, getting hotter and hotter.

"Maria," called a small voice. Guido's wife, Liounna, was waving from the doorway of the newspaper shop. We pushed our way across to her and, without so much as a handshake or a kiss, she led us away from the crowds and to the back of the shop. "Such a crowd," she said as she opened the door into the owner's kitchen and motioned us out the back door to a little laneway made for bicycles and pedestrians. A Vespa came roaring toward us; we stepped into a doorway. When we stepped back onto the street, Liounna was already halfway across someone's terrace. We reached the dead-end street where the local boys were usually involved in a pickup soccer game. Today there was no one.

"The children are at the public garden. There are rides from Rome today," said Liounna.

"At the top of the hill?"

"Sì."

"How on earth did they get the rides up there?"

"Donkeys." Guido was sitting under the shade of his quince tree. Their kitchen window was open to the yard, so, as I arranged the espresso cups on the tray, I could hear Bob telling Guido all about the argument. "The woman lives at number 13 *via Regina Margherita* but the basket seller is a foreigner from Morolo."

"Ey," called Liounna. "I'm from Morolo."

I brought the coffee tray and Liounna carried the olive-oil cake out to the yard.

"They never settled who had the right to sell in that spot," said Bob. "The man from Morolo has a permit —"

"Permits," scoffed Guido. "That's a North American idea. It'll never catch on in Supino."

Sitting in Guido's yard, I could hear the wind pass through the branches of the quince tree and the scratch of the chickens in the back garden. It was easy to forget the crowds here.

"Stay away from the centre of town when the *festa* is on, Bob," warned Guido. "Too many strangers trying to cheat you with fake leather and cheap shirts."

"There's a Mass for San Cataldo," said Liounna.

"Even pickpockets go to church," replied Guido. "Later, you watch the fireworks, Maria. Your father always loved the fireworks."

"What time?"

"When the sky's black."

Guido had been a young boy when my father was still living in Supino. He'd followed my dad and his calf along the trails that led to the mountain of Santa Serena. My father had taught Guido how to let the calf lead the way because the calf avoided the stinging nettles and thistles along the path, how to bend the springtime willow branches into a cone shape to trap a wild songbird, how to whittle a divining rod and use it to find water, how to make a cross from the palm leaves given by the priest on Palm Sunday, and where to find the first blue flowers of the springtime up on Santa Serena to pick and take back home to Mama.

"Where's Kathryn today?" asked Guido.

"The *festa*," replied Liounna. "Young people don't mind crowds."

"When there's too many people, I can't breathe," said Guido, and he started to cough at the very mention of the crowds. Liounna reached through the open window for his puffer.

"Once we get here, we never see Kathryn," I said. "She's always off with her Supino friends."

"Why you worry?" asked Liounna. "Caterina's okay. She was here this morning with Davide, your neighbour boy. They brought me some lemons from Sorrento that they found at the market. And some fresh ricotta. Tomorrow we're going to make ravioli, Caterina and I."

"Always a special feast for San Cataldo," explained Guido. "Your father liked that too."

"Let's grab a loaf of bread on the way home," said Bob as we left my cousin's place.

I reminded him that Guido had said to stay away from the centre of the village.

"We'll detour through the back lane."

We entered the bread bakery through the back door and were immediately crushed into a slow-moving queue. With our loaf finally tucked safely under Bob's arm, we turned to retrace our steps. Then, a loud boom. Another explosion followed. Before we knew it, we were out on the street, surrounded by Supinese and strangers, staring at the puffs of smoke that billowed from the mountainside.

"Fireworks?" I said, even though it was mid-afternoon.

"Cannonballs," said the baker.

"Where on earth would someone find cannonballs in Supino?"

"Left over from the war."

The bells from San Sebastiano rolled up the hill with the crowd; bells from the other three churches tumbled down to meet us. The cannonballs continued to boom as we surged up to the Church of San Pietro. One thousand villagers squashed into a piazza that could accommodate 500. Every balcony that overlooked the square was packed with bodies and hung with satin ribbons of gold and burgundy. The church doors opened, emitting the trace of incense, the song of praise to San Cataldo, and a cart crammed with candles.

My father had told me that the candles for San Cataldo were fat as salamis and, once they were lit, their wax dripped onto the cobblestones, making the streets as slick as ice. I watched as the candles passed from hand to hand and altar boys with equally long tapers lit the wicks. The women, cradling the fat candles in their arms, continued their song of praise as they led the procession down the hill, to the Church of San Sebastiano.

My father had told me about this church too, the smallest in Supino, where the priest liked to walk along the path of beech trees every afternoon before the six o'clock Mass. We followed the women carrying the dripping candles and the red-robed men who carried the platform with the statue of San Cataldo, his gold cross shining in the noonday sun. The procession passed by the vendors with their covered wares and arrived at the bottom of the street, where the village priest, flanked by altar boys, walked to the podium. Although the sound system ensured that everyone could hear the prayers and the homilies, the priest seemed uncomfortable with the microphone and loudspeakers. I too was uncomfortable — with the crowd, the bored vendors waiting for the sign that they could uncover their goods, and the unfamiliar faces that lined our streets. I empathized with Guido, who said he couldn't breathe during the festival days.

We worked our way to the side of the Kennedy Bar where a laneway ran parallel to the main street. That's where we met Kathryn and Davide.

"What are you doing here?" we said to each other.

"Heading home," I said.

"Heading out of town," said Kathryn.

"Too much chaos," said Davide.

We spent the rest of the day at our house, mostly in the tiny backyard. At dinnertime we ate tomato sandwiches. I made coffee in our little espresso pot on our hot plate. Bob ate the last of the *ginette* cookies and their anisette-flavoured icing broke off in flakes, landing on the patio. We sat quietly as the late-day sparrows arrived to carry off the sweet crumbs. Toward evening we moved to the balcony and watched strangers trudging up our street with babies sleeping in arms, children carried on backs, parcels tucked beneath arms or stuffed into shopping bags, back to cars double-parked on our street.

As the sun disappeared behind Santa Serena, we carried our bed to the open window. I said, "I'm going to pretend I'm sitting on the roof of my dad's farmhouse, like he always did, and watch the fireworks."

"I'll be back in a minute," said Bob.

When he returned, he held a tray containing two tumblers of vermouth and a little white bag. "To your father," he said, lifting the glass. I opened the bag filled with my favourite candies, miniature licorice allsorts. "Found them at the market," said Bob.

Supinese fireworks burst across the sky. Flares shot up and cascaded into fountains of sparkling confetti. A streak of lightning yellow flew across the black sky, scattering a thousand tiny lemon drops. A red ball burst into a green ball and into a yellow flame that sizzled as it spiralled. Between the bursts, the village dogs barked, and the donkey, who lived across the ravine, brayed in response. I remember that sparkling night with the scent of smoke in the air and the damp evening breeze and the comforting feel of Bob's shoulder leaning against mine.

The next morning, we opened our balcony shutters to silence. The vendors, the visitors, and the festival excitement had left the village. Benito was sweeping our street, our next-door neighbour Sam was setting up scaffolding to begin retiling his roof, and Angela was leaning out her kitchen window watching. Davide's motorcycle was idling outside our house.

"We're going over to Guido and Liounna's," said Kathryn. "Why don't you come for lunch later. We're making ravioli."

Since we wouldn't be in the village for Joe and Angela's 25th wedding anniversary party in September, we took the gift we'd bought in Venice over to their house on the afternoon of our last day. We also took half a loaf of bread.

"Why you keep buying a loaf?" Joe asked. "I told you. Say 'Mezzo,' and they cut the loaf in half for you."

I didn't explain that we'd purposely bought a whole loaf so we'd have mezzo to give to Angela and Joe in exchange for all the eggs and vegetables and fruits left on our doorstep.

"We wanted to give you this little gift for your anniversary," said Bob, and Joe handed the box to Angela.

"Bella," she said, unpacking each of the glasses and setting them up on her sideboard. "Why don't you stay for the party. My relatives come from L'Aquila for three days. My cousin, she makes that spaghetti that Bob likes — alla carbonara."

"I'd like to," Bob said, and he paused for a moment as if he was seriously considering staying on for a few months just to eat homemade spaghetti alla carbonara. "But I have my business and Maria goes back to class in September. Kathryn too. We'll be back next summer."

"Next summer, we got to find the good door for the backyard. That door we got now is too thin," said Joe. "And Maria said she doesn't like those patio tiles that I put, even if they are free. She wants terra cotta. Mamma mia. That's gonna cost some money, Bob. Also Maria said she doesn't like that light

I hung in the living room. Says those little mirrors are too bright. I said they're supposed to be bright, that's the point. How you like an awning for the backyard? Benito says the man who sells at the market is going to buy a new one. She's a little faded but still good for shade. Also, there's the Feast of San Lorenzo next August. I put your name for the decorating committee." Joe put up his hand. "You don't need to speak Italian, Bob. Just hang a few dozen banners. Put some ribbons from house to house. You know, crisscross. Won't take more than a few hours one morning. The city brings the ladders. We take it all down the next day. You know that guy from Pennsylvania? He comes for the whole summer, April till September. Brings his family. Even brings his American car — what you call that? Station wagon."

"Too bad you don't stay for the party," said Angela. "How you feel if my cousins live at your house for a few days? I take care of everything."

Five

The next summer, we discovered we needed to spend more time in the village because now our patio was missing — only six stones still stood in a drunken tower where the patio had been. Someone had dug two trenches: one ran 10 feet toward the ravine and the second went toward the right for another 10 feet to Peppe's house next door. Our patio was stranded in the middle.

I stood in the doorway trying to take it all in: the uprooted banana tree, which Benito had planted for us as a shade tree, now teetered on the edge of the ravine, its roots bound in a cotton sack that looked suspiciously like my book bag. The rosemary bush, the roses, the laurel bush, and all the other plants Benito had crammed into our tiny garden were now stuffed into plastic pails lining the bottom of the trenches. A small backhoe perched precariously on the pile of excavated dirt and rocks. If the backhoe tipped over, it would go tumbling into the ravine, taking the banana tree with it.

"What on earth?" I said. From across the ravine, the rooster crowed. Benito came around the corner, through Sam's yard and into ours with a bucket and began to dole out cupfuls of water to his plants. I heard him clucking over a brown leaf here, a broken branch there. He gave us a wave and whistled for his brother. Two minutes later Joe was in the yard.

"Don't worry, Maria," said Joe. "Sam from next door — he explained everything before he dug the trenches so Benito could move his plants."

"But what are the trenches for?"

"Sam's building a wall to keep the soil from falling into the ravine at the back. He's going to extend it right across the back of his house and yours. See those rocks over there? He's going to use them."

"A wall's not a bad idea," said Bob. "You don't want the patio to slowly slide into the ravine."

"Look, Joe," I said, "tell him we're only here for a few weeks each summer and couldn't he build the wall later?"

"He's got the backhoe for another job so might as well do it now," Joe explained.

"But we don't have anywhere to . . ."

There was no point in saying we didn't have anywhere to sit, because Joe had already told us to sit on his patio. He had the afternoon shade.

"Sam's not charging you for the work — not even for the stones," said Joe. "He wants to know, though, what about the space underneath your patio?"

"You mean the dirt under our patio? What about it?"

"Sam has a plan to use it for a cantina. Dig it out sort of like a cave. It would be cool under there and good for storing wine or apples and potatoes in the winter."

"How would we get into the cantina?" I asked. There were no steps from our patio into the yard, and even if there were, we'd then be in Sam's yard. Our backyard consisted of a 10-foot-by-10-foot patio, accessed from our back door, and nothing more.

"Why you want to go in Sam's cantina? Listen, Maria, let me explain to you again. Sam will build the stone wall and he'll put in a new patio for you. He's looking for some old — what's that word? authentic — when Sam finds some authentic terra cotta tiles he'll get Mario, the old bricklayer, to lay them. Don't worry, Mario does good work. He's an artisan. Sam's going to put a wrought-iron fence too so you can't fall off the patio. Then Benito needs a little space for his pots and you'll still have lots of room to sit."

I thought about my cousin Guido and his advice: whoever owns the grapevine owns the grapes that grow there. If Sam builds a cantina under our patio, he'll own the cantina but the cantina will be on our land. How long does a cantina have to stand before the land belongs to the cantina owner? And did it even matter, since we had no use for the soil beneath our patio anyway?

Lorenzo the barber had told us about a man who owned a narrow three-storey house in Supino Centro. There were matching houses on both sides with single-car garages on the street level. The owner moved to the States and left the house empty. "The man who stayed in Supino knocked out the inside wall between his garage and the *Americano*'s garage and parked his car there. Also a Vespa," said Lorenzo. "Ten years passed, maybe 15. Finally the *Americano* comes back to Supino. Maybe he's going to fix up his house. Maybe he's thinking to sell, I don't know. What does the *Americano* find when he opens his garage door? The neighbour's car. Then he sees there's no wall between his garage and next door's. Just one big garage. The *Americano* starts yelling and swearing. Tells the Supinese to get his bloody car out of his garage. Tells him to rebuild the wall. The Supinese says he's used the space for 10 years. In Supino, if you take care of something for 10 years it belongs to you."

I don't know if it's a real law or just a Supinese inter-pretation of the law, but Lorenzo said the garage man's car remains in the narrow neighbour's garage. When I asked what happened to the *Americano*, Lorenzo just shrugged. "He left."

"Sam can't dig a cantina for himself underneath our patio," I said. "We own that land."

"He's going to trade. The cantina for the terra cotta patio and the iron fence," explained Joe. He spoke slowly so we'd understand.

"We don't need a patio . . ." I began, but looking around at the leaning tower of patio stones, I realized that we did need a patio. "Let me think about it."

Bob and I discussed it over coffee, we discussed it over pizza, we discussed it under the Big and Little Dippers out-side our bedroom window, and we discussed it while sitting on Joe's patio, beneath the shady grapevines, in the after-noon. It came down to a few basic points: It was our land.

We wanted an authentic terra cotta patio and a wrought-iron fence. We had no use for the land underneath our patio since we couldn't access it. It was our land.

"We're only here for a few weeks every summer," I said, but we couldn't decide whether that meant we should allow Sam to build the patio so we'd have somewhere to sit or, since we were only Summer Supinese, Sam was taking advantage of us and our land beneath our patio, which we didn't have anymore.

We tried to talk it over with Guido, sitting on his patio beneath the quince tree, but he just shook his head throughout the whole conversation and at the end he simply said, "No."

"That's it?" I asked. I had been hoping for some advice.

"No," he repeated. "You need to change the lock on your front door every few years as well or someone can claim that since they have the key to the house, they own it."

After my father's death, I'd begun to write down the stories of Supino that he'd told me, but he'd never mentioned anything about grapevine ownership or the occupation of deserted houses. Bob felt the problem was that we were only visitors to the village, and the solution was for us to spend more time in Italy.

"You've been listening to Joe too much," I said.

"I've been thinking of opening a coffee bar," said Bob. "I could run it in the summer and we'd close in the winter. That would keep me busy all summer."

"What about the rest of the year?"

"I could deliver meals for Meals on Wheels."

"And the coffee company?"

"I'm thinking of selling it."

It sounded like a pipe dream. A dream so fanciful that it was impossible. As unlikely as a couple returning from their first trip to Italy and deciding to buy a house, sight unseen, just because it was in her father's village. Trusting a stranger in the village to oversee the renovations and have the house livable for 10 days in August when they'd take her father back to his birthplace after 64 years away. Now believing that the magic that was Supino could last for the entire summer. Without the coffee company, we'd have the time to spend summers in Supino, but we'd also be without an income. Still, the idea settled into our minds and it became less an impossible dream than a challenge that we might solve.

We were too young to retire, but not old enough to settle for security. Bob knew coffee; in Toronto he imported green coffee beans, and he had a staff who roasted and packaged them for delivery to restaurants. He was good with people, so he'd enjoy running a coffee shop. He'd have to learn the language, but Joe could help him with the permits and the set-up. Kathryn may have sparked some of this thought because she'd found a Canadian high school in Italy and had already applied to complete her final semester there. It wasn't in Supino, of course, but it was less than two hours away.

Bob signed up for a Berlitz intensive Italian course and went faithfully twice a week. He bought the books and tapes, and I could often hear him practicing in his home office, but whenever I entered the room, he stopped.

"Speak Italian to me," I'd say, but Bob was reluctant.

"I can understand what people are saying," he said, "but I can't speak."

I felt the opposite: that given a few minutes I could put together a grammatically correct Italian sentence, matching the adjectives to the gender of the nouns and selecting the correct verb tense and level of familiarity. "I'm okay to speak," I said, "but when the person answers, especially if they speak fast, I'm lost."

"Then we make a good team," Bob said.

Through that winter, Bob went to Italian class and I wrote weekly vocabulary lists and memorized them. One week it was lists of fruits and vegetables, the next week clothing, the following week common questions. Now that Bob could understand more Italian, he became increasingly involved in the Toronto Supino Social Club. He was the treasurer and attended the monthly meetings. The group's main priority was to buy a clubhouse.

"The committee put a down payment on an unfinished unit in Woodbridge," Bob told me. "Now we have to finish the unit so we can host some fundraisers to pay the mortgage."

"You could rent a hall to hold a fundraiser."

"Why would we rent when we already own? The unit just needs a little work."

"Are you hiring a contractor?"

"Why would we hire a contractor? The Supinese know how to do the work. First, we call a meeting and tape up some bristol board. We write one job on each board — plumbers, electricians, carpenters, drywall installers, tile layers, painters. People sign up according to their skill. Then we'll serve coffee and cake."

"What if a member can't do any of those things?"

"Most of the Supinese can do *all* of those things. Those of us who aren't tradespeople will donate in a different way. For example, the barbers have already said they'd pay for the light fixtures. I'm donating the coffee equipment."

"How are you going to make coffee for the meeting without electricity?"

"I'll brew it at the coffee company and bring it in the big urn. Paper cups, stir sticks — I can bring all that."

"There's no heat in the building."

"People can leave their coats on."

"You know, you're starting to sound like Joe," I said.

"Thanks."

Then one Tuesday night in March, the phone rang and everything changed. "That was the police," Bob told me. "There's been an accident with your mother. She's had some sort of stroke and crashed her car. An ambulance is taking her to the hospital."

Humber Memorial Hospital was a six-minute walk from our house; I was at the emergency entrance in four. "Josie Coletta," I said, and they said they couldn't find her. I explained about the police and the phone call, and somewhere in the back of my mind I held on to the idea that it was all a mistake and they'd phoned the wrong number. Maybe it was a different Josie Coletta with a daughter named Maria who had the same phone number as me.

"She's en route to North York General," said the nurse, and I was out the door.

Kathryn was just pulling into the driveway as I ran up the front walk. I got in the passenger side. "Do you know where North York General is?"

We were at the hospital in 40 minutes, and even though my mother was there in the emergency ward, we had to sit in the waiting room. I phoned my brother and my sister only to say that I was at the hospital but I didn't know any-thing about mom's condition. Time dragged by. I paced. I checked in with the emergency-room receptionist so many times she started shaking her head as soon as she saw me heading her way.

"See that door?" I said to Kathryn. "I'm pretty sure it's an exit from the emergency ward. We could just slip in there when no one's looking."

'Which door?" said Kathryn. She sounded willing.

"The one marked 'No Entry.'"

I don't remember how I got into the emergency ward but I do remember standing beside the bed where my mother lay. Her speech was blurred. Technicians and nurses kept coming in to run tests. I overheard someone say that in these stroke cases the first 24 hours are crucial, and if it's the right kind of stroke they can administer a drug that works wonders. Did my mother have the right kind of stroke? My brother and sister had arrived by then, but all we could do was wait. More nurses and technicians, in and out, blood pressure and blood tests and reflexes tests and talk about x-rays and the question "Has the specialist arrived yet?" It all sounded hopeful.

Someone put a fat folder on the counter of the nurses' station. A doctor flipped through the pages, shaking her head, and then she came to our mother's bedside. Mom's eyes were closed, but I thought she was still conscious. I held her hand and said, "I'm here."

"Massive stroke," began the doctor. "If she survives the first 24 hours, we'll see if she can survive 48."

My mother squeezed my hand.

Because there were no other beds available, my mother spent almost a week in the emergency ward, and every morning when I arrived, I spoke to her as if she were still conscious and lucid and, really, just resting. I don't think either of us was fooled. Bob and Kathryn came to the hospital after work every night, bringing dinner. We sat beside my mother's bed and talked and ate and tried to pretend everything was normal.

Finally they moved her to a room, which we decorated with drawings from the grandchildren and flowers and helium balloons so she could see that she was loved, if only she'd open her eyes. Her brothers and sisters and friends and cousins all came, spending five minutes here and five minutes there, each one speaking to her, but my mother never answered. She couldn't swallow, she couldn't speak, she couldn't move her left leg, she got a kidney infection, she caught pneumonia, and she didn't open her eyes.

On the 21st day, the fingers on her left hand began to turn black and the hand grew cold, and the doctor said, "Circulation problem." Then the doctor said, "Amputation." And my mother didn't open her eyes. The doctor asked me if they could amputate my mother's arm.

I closed my eyes. A nurse came floating into my mother's room; she said her name was Fatima. She said she had a message for me. "At least do no harm."

I said, "No amputation." The following day, I said, "No IV." We'd already signed the Do Not Resuscitate order. We were back to waiting.

After 23 days in hospital, my mother died.

I found a funeral home featuring a central staircase and red velvet curtains. "I think my mother would like this place," I said to Bob. "It's kind of fancy and she liked that style. I was thinking about those girlfriends that she used to work with at Toronto Macaroni, 60-odd years ago, who kept phoning to see how she was doing. The grandchildren have no idea of what Mom was like when she was young. Did you know she learned to ride a bike when I was 12? She would have been 42. She said she never had a chance to learn before. I can still see her whizzing down the sidewalk with her dark black curls and her sweater flying out behind her. The grandchildren only know the woman who shopped at the dollar stores and studied the grocery flyers for the best prices and slipped them 20 dollars when it was their birthday. They don't know about the young Josie Coletta who worked in the office at Toronto Macaroni."

"Why don't you tell them?" said Bob. "You can speak at the funeral."

"I can't speak. I'll break down and cry."

"It wouldn't matter if you did. But you can speak. You can do anything when you really want to."

So I met with the priest who was to say the funeral Mass
and asked permission to speak. "Yes," he said. "I see here
on the death certificate that your mother was born in
Greensburg, Pennsylvania."

"Yes," I said. "Her parents emigrated from Colliano,
Italy, and she was born in Greensburg. Then her mother
died in the influenza epidemic of 1918 and her father took
the children back to Italy. Later they emigrated again, this
time to Canada."

All the time I was reciting my family history, droning on
and on, I was wondering what difference it made where my
mother was born.

"I was ordained in Greensburg," said the priest. "Your
mother has travelled far from her birthplace. It's time to
send her to her eternal home."

So after the priest began the Mass, I spoke about my
mother. I spoke clearly and calmly about a vibrant woman
who once wore stockings with a line down the back and fash-
ionable hats and suits and fire-engine-red lipstick. I talked
about the stylish woman who worked at Toronto Macaroni
with the other girls, who painted her fingernails red and
smoked cigarettes and went to the opera or dancing at the
Palais Royale on Saturday nights. I didn't cry — not until I
sat back down and the singer began *"Ave Maria."*

Although my mother was not born in Supino, members
of the Toronto branch of the Supino Social Club came to
the funeral. At the end of her life, the Supinese were there,
reciting Italian prayers at her funeral Mass.

We'd lived next door to my parents, in the town of
Weston, for more than 20 years. After my mother's death,

Bob and I removed the little path of patio stones that led from our front door to theirs and filled in the squares with sod. I talked about moving, but Bob said we shouldn't make any decisions for at least a year. We knew that death could make you think you're sane when really you're not. My brother and sister and I sorted out the things from our parents' house. Bob brought cardboard boxes from the coffee company and we divided up the dishes and pots and pans; we also piled up boxes for charity, gave away the furniture, and gave our mother's costume jewellery to the grandchildren as mementos.

The following summer we spent three weeks in the village. We did the usual things, walking daily to the shops in the morning and to the water fountain in the afternoon. Our part of the street was narrow, but once you got to the end of our block, the street widened; city workers spent that summer laying sidewalks from that section all the way to the water fountain. They arranged cobblestones in consecutive arches that matched the curve of the street. They installed streetlights as well. The sides of the street were still dense with saplings, Queen Anne's lace, and the occasional songbird.

We attended the watermelon festival that summer as well as a celebration of fettuccine. When we ate meals at Guido's little farmhouse, we brought flowers or pastries. It didn't seem like enough though, so one day we invited Guido and Liounna to come to the restaurant at the Hotel Dalma for all-you-can-eat pizza.

"All you can eat?" repeated Liounna.

"A North American idea," said Guido. "That guy from Detroit with his big ideas. Eat like a pig so you can brag about it? Makes no sense. Anyway, it's too far to walk."

We had planned to drive to the restaurant on the outskirts of Supino, but we didn't press him.

The restaurant's owner, Riccardo, spoke English, as long as you were talking about food. There was no menu: he recited his specials: "Linguine, fettuccine, spaghetti with meat-a-ball or *salsicce* — how you say? — sausage, and beef-a steak-a, and *pollo*, what you call chicken. And pig slices." That would be pork chops.

This summer he added a sign to the front of his hotel that advertised all-you-can eat pizza on Saturday nights. He'd set up a few patio tables and plastic lawn chairs on a small patch of grass below the sign — enough room for about 10 customers. That's where we were sitting. In the adjacent garden the owner's son played on his swing set and his nephew sat beside the ornamental pond, trying to catch the goldfish.

"Why you sit here?" asked Riccardo.

"Pizza," said Bob, pointing to the sign.

"Follow me."

We trooped through the empty dining room, past the noisy kitchen, all steam and tangy tomato sauce, and straight out the kitchen door into the backfield. A dog lounged under the shade of the hotel laundry. Obviously Riccardo had misunderstood us and was taking us on a tour of his property. "Here she is!" he said with a majestic sweep of his arm. A good 80 metres beyond the restaurant, over the field dotted with dandelions and plantain, was a clearing, about the size of our Toronto backyard. Riccardo had set up three blue canvas canopies there. We walked on a path lined with buttercups, their faces as shiny as shellac. Beneath two canopies were tables set with linen cloths and wildflowers of pale purple. There were chairs for maybe 40 people. Beneath the third canopy was a long table laden with stacks of china plates, cloth napkins, wine and water glasses, and a large plastic tub of olives. Wicker torches fenced the area.

Bob said, "This is pretty far from your kitchen."

"I can use the exercise," said Riccardo, patting his generous stomach.

"But every week you have to carry everything out here," said Bob. "What if it rains?"

Riccardo pointed vaguely to his son and nephew and dog. "I have assistants. The last day it rained in Supino was on a Tuesday. We are open in the pizza field only on Saturday night." Riccardo stopped at the first table and pulled out a chair. "Is this all right?" he asked. We were the only customers. He whipped out a small notebook and a pencil. "May I take your order?"

In the field next door, a dog yelped. Bells began to clunk and clatter as the dog directed a flock of sheep from the clover pasture onto the street, and a shepherd stood in the middle of the road, waving his crook. The bells, the dog's barks, and the bleats of the sheep made it impossible to speak to Riccardo, so we waited. We watched as an approaching car screeched to a stop, and the sound spooked the sheep so that some returned bleating to the clover pasture while others ran, bells jangling, down the roadway. This resulted in more barks from the dog and a few curses from the shepherd. By the time the sheep were safely corralled into their field, another family had made the trek out from the dining room to the pizza field and Riccardo had left our table to seat them.

The sun was glowing rosy red across the wildflowers, casting long shadows beyond the laundry, where a woman pulled off wooden clothes pegs and folded the clothes into a large wicker basket. I watched her fade into a shadow in the twilight, and then it was dark. I could barely see Bob's face across the table. That's when Riccardo's nephew began to light the torches that edged the field.

"Allora," said Riccardo, returning to our table, "what will it be?"

Bob ordered in his newly learned Berlitz Italian, *"Vino rosa e pizza con peperoni."*

Riccardo wagged his index finger. "No, *signor* Bob," he said, *"peperoni* is peppers and you don't like peppers. You want *salsiccia piccante.* That's spicy sausage, in English."

"His English is better than my Italian," said Bob.

"Only with food," I assured Bob. "You just need practice."

Riccardo's son, who was about 10, approached the table with a dish of olives and a beer glass holding bread sticks. He was back a few minutes later to pour red wine from a pottery jug. *"Vino di papa mio,"* he explained. Now that Riccardo's nephew had lit all the torches, we could see the perimeter of the pizza field as well as the path that led to the back door of the restaurant. The buttercups had tucked their faces beneath their leaves and settled down for the night.

Riccardo, with plates of pizza up one arm and down the other, ran this pathway dozens of times that evening. Our pizzas were still bubbling hot when he sat them on the table. We stayed a long time. The pizza crust was so thin that even though we'd both eaten a pizza the size of a dinner plate, we were willing to try a second. Riccardo recommended a white pizza with artichokes since they were in season. The artichokes were drizzled with olive oil and grated garlic. We drank a second bottle of wine.

"It's endearing in its own crazy way, isn't it?" said Bob. "Eating pizza in the middle of some farmer's field."

"It's different, I'll give it that," I said. "In most places you don't have to wait for the sheep bells to stop clanging so you can order. And in Toronto, you'd never get away with using 10- and 12-year-olds as waiters. I don't see how Riccardo can make any money charging 10 bucks for all-you-can-eat pizza."

"That's not the point," said Bob. "He wanted to try something new and he did."

"You're always assessing restaurants in Toronto. You're always telling me about location and experience and competitive pricing."

"That's business."

"This is business too, Bob."

"It's a different business sense here. Look at Riccardo. His family owns this land — probably owned it for generations — so instead of grazing sheep or planting wheat, the family built the hotel and the restaurant. He's not renting the place — or, as your father would have said, 'Throwing money out the window on rent.' A few hotel guests each night and a few customers in the restaurant and he's doing okay. The thing is, he's enjoying it. If the all-you-can-eat pizza doesn't pan out, maybe he'll try pizza delivery. You know, that's not a bad idea."

"Joe would say, 'Why you need delivery? You just walk to the place and buy.'"

"Joe's only thinking about Supino Centro. It could work out here in the suburbs."

"Is it really 11:30?" I asked, pulling on my sweater. "Let's get the bill."

As we got up to leave, I realized that all the tables were full, but the voices of our neighbouring diners distilled across the pizza field, their stories travelling next door to the sheep now asleep in their field. Riccardo's nephew was right beside us — *"Momento,"* he said, and he pulled a torch from the ground and led the way back to the parking lot.

Six

Electricity in Italy is expensive, so that summer we tried once again to sort out our hydro bill. Originally, our travel agent had arranged to have our hydro turned on for us. That's when our problems began, because according to Frosinone hydro logic, our travel agent had requested the activation of the hydro for our house and therefore the travel agent received the bill. Since the travel agent paid the bill (and we then paid him), the hydro company believed the travel agent owned the house. Not only had the hydro officials classified our house as the travel agent's second home, they charged a higher rate for the hydro for our house.

When we showed Joe the bill, he said, "It's crazy to pay so much. I shut off the hydro."

"Joe, we need hydro."

"Those guys in Frosinone with their sit-down jobs. How many times you have to tell them that you own the house?

I run the electric cord from my house to your house while you're here. When you leave, you give me a few dollars."

"Maybe we better keep things the way they are until we can get the bill changed to our name."

"Better I put the cord from my house to yours."

"Is that legal?"

"Legal?" repeated Joe, as if he wasn't familiar with the word.

Joe ran a fluorescent orange hydro cord from his upstairs bedroom window across the street to our balcony. The cord was so bright it practically glowed. Anyone walking or driving down our street could see that we were sharing electricity.

"This is dangerous," I said to Bob. "If someone from Frosinone hydro sees the cord we're going to be fined, and without hydro."

"We'll explain that it's temporary."

"We can't even explain that we own the house."

"Let me talk to Peppe about it, see what he says."

Our next-door neighbour Peppe did not speak English, but he and Bob had struck up a friendship using Bob's Berlitz School Italian. Peppe would take Bob off to some bar or another in Supino and they'd talk. I was never part of this arrangement, although Bob would tell me Peppe's stories when he got back home. Peppe was a businessman. He owned a car-parts dealership in the next town and a chestnut grove on the mountain. His parents lived on a farm near the base of the Santa Serena mountain; his family had always lived in Supino and they always would. Peppe was a widower — his wife had died several years before and he was raising two teenagers on his own. The older one was Davide, the boy with whom Kathryn spent most of her days and evenings, often on the back of his motorcycle.

Someone in the suburbs of Supino had just opened a bar that summer in the main floor of their house. That's where Bob and Peppe had their coffee and conversation. "A good size bar with eight tables," Bob told me. "And they turned their driveway into a patio where they could seat more customers."

"Where did the customers park?"

"Wherever," said Bob, making the circular gesture. "Peppe thinks you should always make a business in your own house. Never rent. If you don't have enough room, or your wife doesn't want to turn her living room into a bar, then you have to buy."

"We are not turning our living room into a bar for the summer," I said. "I don't care what Peppe and Joe say."

"Joe says that empty lot between Sam's place next door and Carlo, the mechanic's shop, would make a good patio."

"Mario across the street owns that land."

"Not necessarily."

"He's got a vegetable garden there."

"That's because he doesn't have enough room in his own yard. Listen, Joe says there's a place for sale at the piazza of San Pietro. It's a three-level house. I could have a bar on the main floor and rent out the upstairs rooms. The rent would eventually pay for the house."

"I don't know, Bob. It's one thing to buy a house for ourselves, but to buy with the idea of opening a business . . ."

"Don't worry. We're just going to look. No one said anything about buying. But doesn't the location sound good?
Right on the piazza, with parking directly in front of the
church and no competition. Think of the possibilities . . ."

"Did you get anywhere with the hydro?"

"Yeah, Peppe agrees with Joe that it's an outrageous
amount to pay for hydro, especially since we're Summer
Supinese. He thinks you're right too. It's dangerous to run
the extension cord across the street. He says it's just a matter
of time before some snoopy official starts asking questions."

"But did he have a solution?"

"Sure, he said we'll run the cord out the back window
from his house and into our back bedroom window. No one
will see it."

On Thursday mornings there was a huge outdoor market in
Frosinone, about half an hour away. Kathryn particularly
liked the shoe vendors who arranged their shoes in towers
by price — 10 euro, 15 euro, etc. — and all you had to do was
find your size. We often went there early in the morning,
just to browse. Sometimes we'd buy something for Angela:
buffalo mozzarella from Salerno or pineapples from Sicilia
that you'd never find in Supino. After the market, we'd stop
at Rendezvous, the take-out pizza shop in Frosinone, where
they displayed thick pizza baked on cookie sheets and the
woman cut the pizza with scissors and weighed the slices on
her scale. After that we'd go to the newsstand in the middle
of the parking lot, where Bob would buy a Rome paper so he
could practice reading Italian.

That Thursday morning, as we approached the *autostrada*, where we'd cross over into the city of Frosinone, I said, "Why don't we drive down to Vietri sul Mare? It's not that far."

"I told Joe we were going to the market."

"We'll be back by dinner."

"Hold on," said Bob, and he made a U-turn onto the *autostrada* heading south. We left the windows open as we sped along; Bob had to shout to be heard. "I figure we can make it in about two hours. I wouldn't mind spending a bit of time in Naples. Maybe next time we could spend the night."

"Sure, if we got permission from Joe and the neighbours," I said.

"They're just watching out for us so we don't miss any of the summertime activities. By the way, they're closing the street in front of the three telephone booths and setting up chairs there. Joe said he and Benito are putting torches on the wall above the phone booths and stringing plastic flags. I thought I'd give them a hand if we're back in time. There's a jazz band performing tonight."

"You don't even like jazz particularly."

"That's not the point," he said. "It's important to go to these activities. We don't want people sitting inside watching television every night. Even if I'm not a jazz fan, I enjoy being involved."

"You know what, Bob? You're becoming Italian."

"Thanks," said Bob, and he reached over and patted my leg. "Do you still want to buy those tiles for the kitchen?"

"Yes, and maybe I'll look at their hand-painted dishes."

I didn't need dishes, but my mother had had a soft spot for china, and since her death I'd somehow picked up her interest and her habit of buying a pretty piece here and there. We drove past Naples and Salerno to my mother's part of Italy. My mother had no happy memories of this place and her sad stories had rubbed off on me so that I'd never considered visiting her village. Her recollections of her childhood in Colliano were hunger and poverty, and even though that was years ago, her impressions were so negative that I too avoided the village where she'd gone hungry.

Vietri sul Mare, on the other hand, was a charming village high above the sea. There potters and painters spent their days creating ceramics. Their main street was full of ceramic shops and tourists, but just a few steps up the hill was the residential area with locals and *trattorias* and young artisans in tiny shops creating unusual pieces. The first thing I bought was a small stoneware tray with six espresso cups and a sugar bowl. Then I bought a jug in the shape of a rooster and four plates of navy blue with yellow lemons. I stood in the corner of the shop watching the painter working on his plates. He had just a few pots of colours on his worktable, which was pushed up tight to the open window, overlooking the sea. When he finished a piece, he signed his name on the bottom in black.

Before leaving, I bought a few bowls because they had cherries painted on them and my mother had been fond of cherries. I also bought a ceramic house plaque for Joe and Angela that had the number 13 in the centre and was bordered with pretty yellow and blue flowers.

"What about the kitchen tiles?" Bob asked.

"I can't decide. We can look again after lunch."

We left the parcels in the car and started walking back

uphill. Joe had warned us never to eat in a restaurant that offered a tourist menu because the food would only be the North American idea of Italian food. "Spaghetti — cooked too much — and meat-a-balls. Always eat where the locals go," said Joe, and when I'd asked him how I would know where the locals ate, he said, "Look around."

So we looked around: the shopkeepers were locking their doors; businesspeople came from upstairs offices. We followed them into the side street where a set of stairs led to an open doorway hung with beaded ropes. Two businessmen went inside. "What do you think?" I asked Bob. *"Scusa,"* said the parking lot attendant as he stepped by us and pushed aside the ropes. Inside, long tables were set for communal dining and, as we hesitated, looking for a hostess or some sign that we were to seat ourselves, more locals pushed in. Bob grabbed my hand, then grabbed two chairs, and we sat. Water, wine, and bread were already on the table.

A woman came from the kitchen with plates of antipasto and put one on each table. After a few minutes she returned with bowls of penne in tomato sauce and a small dish of grated romano. A younger woman collected the empty pasta bowls. Then they brought several platters: roasted potatoes with rosemary sprigs, peas, and *prosciutto*, and thin slices of veal with lemon quarters edging the plate. We ate family-style with platters of food passed from hand to hand. Our tablemates poured wine or water and passed the breadbasket. The salad arrived in a large ceramic bowl with ruffled edges. The only choice we had regarding the meal came at the end when the woman offered espresso. There was no bill. We followed the others to the cash desk at the front where everyone was charged the same amount, unless they had espresso, and then they were charged an extra euro.

The shops were closed until four.

"We can walk around a bit, if you want," said Bob. "Or drive down to the beach for an hour."

"Let's head home."

"What about the tiles?"

"Next time."

At the parking lot, the newspaper kiosk was open and Bob bought a cooking magazine, *Sale e Pepe*, for me.

"You don't have to make any of the recipes," he said. "It'll be good for your vocabulary, don't you think?"

"Yes, and I can give the magazine to Angela when we leave."

"No, she'd be insulted. She'd say, 'Why you give me this? You think I don't know how to cook?'"

We took the Amalfi Coast roadway, which hugs the hills on one side and has a guardrail that keeps cars from driving over the cliff on the other. The views were so spectacular that we had to keep pulling over so Bob could take photos. We folded the car's side-view mirrors in and parked mere millimetres from the rocky hillside, then we waited for a break in the traffic before we raced across the road to the guardrail. Even with my knees touching the guardrail, I could feel the swoosh of the traffic at my heels. "No more photos," I said, but then we'd round another bend in the road and we'd see something irresistible — a whitewashed house perched precariously on the side of a cliff, tiers of olive trees carpeted with nets, a parking garage on the rooftop, a tiny strip of pebble beach, a cove of fishing boats, a wisteria vine hanging long and purple, a row of terra cotta rooftops so close together they looked like steps — and we'd risk the traffic to take a closer look and another photo. At one point, we made a wrong turn north of Naples and found ourselves on a beach road instead of the *autostrada*. By then the sun was low. We entered a little beach town called Sperlonga, where we stopped for gas and directions. Bob spoke Italian to the gas attendant.

"There's a good *trattoria* in the town," Bob reported when he returned to the car. "They specialize in fish."

"You don't like fish."

"*You* do. And I can practice ordering *senza pesce*."

It was a tiny *trattoria* with a blue-striped awning and several men at tables out front. The setting sun bathed them in cinematic colour. Inside, the tables sat on marine blue tiles. The whitewashed walls featured photos of the beach. Bob ordered everything in Italian: the seafood platter for me with white wine and some asparagus risotto and roasted chicken with red wine and a bottle of bubbly water.

When Bob finished ordering, the waiter repeated the items quickly and the waiter may have added an item or Bob may have said, "*Sì*..." one time too many times, because the waiter brought everything Bob ordered including a plate of penne. There was a saltshaker on the table but no pepper.

"I think I've got all the variations of the word *pepper* worked out," said Bob. "There's pepperoni and peppers and pepper.

"*Pepe?*" asked Bob.

The waiter said, "*Scusa?*"

"*Pepe.*"

We looked around at the other tables in the hope that one of them would have a peppershaker and we could point it out, but the other tables were bare.

"*Momento,*" said the waiter, and he went back to the kitchen, returning in a few seconds with a puzzled-looking cook. "Peppe," introduced the waiter.

I felt pretty confident that Joe would accept the house tile as a gift. No doubt he had some old tiles hanging around his garage, which he could have painted if he'd wanted a ceramic house number. I was prepared to remind Joe that the tiles were hand-painted by an artisan, and the cost was immaterial because they were a gift.

"Where'd you get these?" asked Joe, turning over the tile to reveal the painter's signature.

"Vietri sul Mare."

"Near Naples? Did you visit your mother's village?"

"Maybe next year," I said.

"Maybe I come with you," said Joe. "I want to see Monte Cassino. They say that on a clear day you can get a good view of Supino from there."

"Ey," said Angela from the kitchen window. "You tell them about tomorrow?"

"All the stores are closed tomorrow. Buy what you need today," said Joe.

"Labour strike?" asked Bob, who'd been reading the Rome newspaper.

"That's for the bigga shots who work in the city. We have no time for that. Tomorrow's August 15 *ferragosto.*"

"A feast day?" asked Bob. How many feasts could one small village have? How many saints? How many festivals of watermelon or artichokes or figs? How many ordinary things to celebrate?

"*Ferragosto* is the hottest day of the summer."

"You celebrate the hottest day of the summer?"

"We get out of town. In the evening there's a meteor shower. Hundreds of meteors all across the sky," said Joe, as if the villagers arranged it. "After the 15th, the air cools down a little. Easier to breathe. How's your cousin Guido doing, Maria? Is he coming tomorrow?"

"Where?"

"*Mamma mia!* What you think we're talking about? You got to pay attention. Tomorrow the stores are closed for *ferragosto*."

"Is there a *festa*?"

"No, it's a pic-a-nic. Guido's coming or no?"

Joe took off his hat and rubbed his head. He looked over at Benito, who just shrugged.

If Angela hadn't called down from the kitchen window, who knows what would have happened. "Listen to me," she began. "August 15th is the hottest day of the year. Nobody stays in the village. Everybody, she packs a pic-a-nic and goes to the mountain. The air up there is good. I hear Guido's got some breathing trouble. Maybe he comes, breathes better. You coming?"

"Yes."

"Okay, don't bother with the tables and chairs," said Joe. "I bring extra."

"What kind of picnic needs tables and chairs?" I asked Bob as we headed to the stores to buy some bread and cheese for sandwiches. We also picked up a few cookies and a bottle of lemonade. The shopkeeper gave us a cardboard box to pack it all in. In the morning, I'd add my red-checkered table-cloth, which we could sit on, and we'd be all set.

"I forgot to ask the time."

"Noon. All picnics start at noon."

Kathryn came into our room around 7 a.m. the next morning. "I can't sleep with all the traffic noise."

We cracked open the balcony doors to view a steady stream of cars heading up *via condotto vecchio*. Many of the cars had bicycles, folded picnic tables, portable barbecues, and beach umbrellas stacked on their roof.

"Everyone in town's going up to the mountain," I said. "We better get moving. Are you coming?"

"Davide's taking me to the beach at Terracina for *ferragoṣto*."

"Do you know what the holiday's for?"

"Something to do with some conquerors who arrived on August 15 and found the city deserted. Italians still get out of town on that day. That's what Davide told me, but at the Kennedy Bar pizza place, Adriana said it's a holiday because it's the hottest day of the year, and after today the weather breaks and the heat's more bearable."

I waved goodbye to Kathryn and Davide from the balcony.

"Davide said he'd like to come to Toronto for a visit next summer, if it's okay with us," said Bob. "She might want to move here eventually, you know."

"I know."

"If I open the summer bar, we'd be here for six months every year anyway. I'll put a special chair and table in the corner and you can bring your computer and be the resident writer."

By the time we got organized and up to the mountain it was mid-morning. We drove until we saw Joe's car parked by a grove of pine trees. A sign said, "La Pineta." We walked on a path of soft needles to a meadow dotted with oak and hazelnut, and here the villagers were set up for *ferragosto*. The men had unfolded tables and chairs and beach umbrellas, and barbecues were smoking. Children with bicycles or beach balls were racing across the field between the trees and back into the sunlit meadow. Women were fussing over picnic baskets and trays covered in aluminum foil. There was an impromptu bocce court, a dartboard nailed to a pine tree, and a large cardboard box full of cantaloupes beneath a shade tree.

There were no amusement rides or jumping pillows, no games of chance or hot dog vendors. Everyone lounged. At noon there was a flurry of activity as the men checked the barbecue coals and the women shook tablecloths and spread them on the tables. Soon the air was ripe with the scent of roasting meat and baking *lasagna*. I watched Angela pull provisions out of boxes and line them up on the table: wine, ginger ale, salad, bread, bowls of vegetables, a round of cheese, *prosciutto* in butcher paper, tubs of olives and marinated mushrooms, sun-dried tomatoes, another loaf of bread . . . a bottle of olive oil. Then she started unpacking the heavy plates and silverware. I thought of the paltry lunch we'd brought and was embarrassed to unpack it.

"Ey," called Joe. "Come. Bob, you turn these *spie-dini*, little bit at a time, I don't want them to cook too fast. Angela, bring me the sausages. Maria, sit down at the table, have some wine."

Between courses, other villagers came by to sample Joe's *spiedini* or share some specialty of their own. Alfredo offered spicy sausages on sticks. Bianca from the Bar Italia passed around some chestnuts soaked in rum.

After lunch, Benito took Bob's arm and led him to the makeshift bocce court. Apparently Bob was on Benito's team.

"I don't know how to play this game," Bob said.

"It's like bowling," said someone.

"It's like French *boules*."

"It's like horseshoes."

"You just throw the ball."

Their team was eliminated in the first round.

"Don't worry about it," said Joe. "You'll do better in the tug-of-war."

While the bocce tournament continued with shouts and curses, Bob spread our tablecloth beneath the shade of a beech. I lay my head in his lap and closed my eyes. Peppe and Joe walked over and sat talking to Bob. Peppe started in Italian, pointing in the direction of his chestnut grove, then Joe translated. "Peppe's got a piece of land on the mountain full of chestnut trees," he said. "In October, he and Davide go up to harvest the chestnuts. They sell them at the market. He wants to know how long you're staying. Do you want to go up for the harvest?"

"We won't be here in October," Bob said. Even though

I was half-asleep I could hear the regret in his voice. "Next year," he said. *"Spero."*

Spero, I hope.

"Okay," said Joe. "And he wants to know about Kathryn."

I was wide-awake now.

"When she goes to school in Lanciano and comes to Supino on the weekend, Peppe says not to worry. He'll take care of her, make sure she's okay."

"Grazie, Peppe," said Bob. "And, Joe, I'd like to see that house that's for sale before we go back to Toronto. No hurry."

Joe knocked on the door the next morning. "You ready?"

His car was parked on the street; we got in and away we went to the piazza of San Pietro to see the house that was for sale. There was actually a red-and-white "For Sale" sign in the window and, on closer inspection, I saw three signs on three levels.

"Are there three apartments for sale?" I asked Joe.

"The owner's gone back to Germany," he said. "But I have the key."

A few years ago we may have asked why Joe had the key to some house belonging to a man in Germany, but now we didn't bother. "The house has three rooms, but the guy had trouble selling it."

This news made me feel better. I was totally unsure about buying a house where Bob could open a summer bar. If no one else wanted to buy the place, there had to be something wrong with it.

"See all the parking spaces?" Bob said. "And the front door opens right onto the piazza — that's good."

The double doors of the house on the ground floor were fronted with wrought-iron gates. Joe unlocked the padlock and pulled open the gates. He put the next key into the front door. When we'd first viewed our house in Supino, the rooms smelled musty from years of being unused. I stepped back in preparation, but the air inside this house was sweet and clear. The house had only one room. It was shaped like a cave. The back wall was part of the mountain rock. Someone had chiselled a series of ledges on the rock wall, among the lichen and a few tenacious weeds.

"Here's where you put the fancy liquor bottles," said Joe. *"Millefiori, grappa, sambuca."*

"Just what I was thinking," said Bob. "And on this wall we could put the counter for the espresso machine and the coffee grinder."

The only other thing in the cave room was a door.

"The bathroom," said Joe, opening the door to a modern bathroom all tiled in white.

"Where's the kitchen?" I asked.

"Follow me," said Joe.

We went back outside to a set of ledges. I'd seen these ledges, which circled around the side of the building, filled with pots of azaleas during the azalea *festa*.

"Be careful," said Joe, as he stepped onto the first ledge. "There's no handrail." The ledge stairs led us to another door. Joe pulled out another key, opened another door. "The kitchen," he said. The room was small. A window, containing the second "For Sale" sign, overlooked the piazza.

"There's no sink," I said. "No refrigerator. No cupboards."

Joe sighed. "The plumbing's there. The electricity's there. We put our own cupboards."

Across the back wall was a set of indoor stairs that led upstairs to the bedroom. Here was another small window and the third "For Sale" sign.

"There you are," said Joe. "Just like I told you. Three-room house. That German guy had a girlfriend back home. No, he was engaged but when he brought the girl to Supino to see the house she said she couldn't live in a place where you had to go outside to climb the stairs to the next room. She went right back to Germany. The guy had a good job here, but what could he do? He went back too. I heard he bought an apartment there, in a building with an elevator, and all the rooms on one floor, like the girlfriend wanted."

"Of course," I said. "No one wants to climb the stairs every time they want to use the bathroom."

"The bathroom at your house is upstairs," said Joe. "This one is downstairs."

"But the stairs are outside, Joe," I said. "What about the wintertime?"

"You put on a sweater."

"It's not like the bathroom is outside," said Bob. "Just the stairs. This room is really a perfect size. Not too big. Enough space for — what do you think, Joe — six tables?"

"Wait a minute. Wait a minute," I said. "How can you rent the two upstairs rooms to someone without a bathroom?"

"There is a bathroom," said Joe and Bob in unison. "They just have to walk down the stairs."

The next day I was sitting on Joe's front step when the

donkey loaded with bags of cement went clumping down the cobblestones. The man leading the donkey tipped his hat. "There's a house they're fixing up," said Joe. "You can see it out your balcony. It's the highest house in Supino Centro so it's the house with the best view and the freshest air. The place was bombed in the war. There's no roof. Some of the walls are missing too. The owner lives and works in Rome and he hired Mario, the contractor, to rebuild. That's why you see the donkey every day. Taking the supplies up to the workers. When the house is finished, the family will spend the summers in Supino."

I had seen the donkey several times a day walking patiently along the street, carrying his load. If a Roman decides to rebuild the highest house in the village so the family can spend the summers in Supino, maybe it isn't so unrealistic for a Canadian to open a summer bar.

"There used to be a castle up on that hill," said Joe. "Long time ago. Medieval times, you know. There are still a few rocks from one corner of the castle — bits and pieces like the tiles down near the hotel. Do you know about that? These two guys were digging for a lost city. Not a real city — a make-believe place. What do you call that? Mythical? So they started digging in the suburbs of Supino, where they thought this city named Ecetra was buried. They didn't find it. Instead they found a Roman bath made of tiles. There's the god Neptune on a cart with seahorses. He's carrying a sceptre. You can walk right down the steps and see the mosaics. Historians and archaeologists from Rome all came to investigate and say they're real. Authentic, I mean."

"When are they open?" I asked.

"You go anytime. It's in a field near the hotel."

"Is there an admission fee?"

Joe just shook his head, but I heard him muttering under his breath, "Admission fee. *Mamma mia!*"

I was telling Bob about this mythical city of Ecetra as we walked down the street that afternoon. A city truck was stopped on the road in front of the building just a few doors from the Bar Italia and workers were hanging a sign. Joe wasn't around, so I couldn't point out the sign to him: he'd say it was a waste of money anyway — "Everyone knows it's the Supino library."

For years, this building had been sitting empty. There had been talk of opening an old folks home, but the Supinese couldn't grasp the North American concept of putting their old people into a home. Any Supinese would say, "I already own a home. Why would I pay money to put my parents *there*?"

It wasn't just the money; the Supinese believe in family staying together in the family home, the more generations the better. What would people think if you abandoned your elders to a home with other people that no one wanted to care for?

Beside the door of the would-be old folks home there was a smaller sign that gave the hours the library would be open. Inside I could hear the sounds of hammers and the rasp of handsaws cutting pine.

"A library in Supino. Things are looking up," I said.

Between the jewellery shop and the Church of Santa Maria Maggiore is a little square. Workers were hanging another sign there.

"What on earth?" I said. This sign was in English; it said, "Internet Café."

"Opening on Friday," said the priest. "There'll be a little *festa* after the six o'clock Mass and the blessing of the café."

If this wasn't enough excitement for one day, when we arrived at the bar they had a new flavour of ice cream. Watermelon was in season. One scoop of juicy red watermelon beside a scoop of dark chocolate: I can still taste it.

On the night before we left Supino, Peppe came to say goodbye and to remind Bob about the chestnut harvest in October. He brought us a very large and very heavy home-made pecorino cheese, which Bob wrapped carefully among his clothes in his suitcase.

"I don't think we're allowed to take food on the plane," I said.

"It's not really food," said Bob. "And it's in the suitcase, not our carry-on, so we're safe."

"But I don't think it's allowed."

"Allowed?" said Bob. "That's a North American idea. It'll never catch on in Supino."

That winter Kathryn went to Lanciano to finish her last semester of high school, and the house in Toronto was lonely and quiet without her. Bob continued with his Berlitz classes and his meetings at the Supino Social Club, while I was working on the book. Then, in the spring, we flew to Lanciano to watch Kathryn graduate before driving up to Supino. Bob brought photos of the newly finished Toronto Supino Social Club to show to Joe and Peppe.

"I told Peppe that it's fine for Davide to stay with us in Toronto next month," said Bob. "But Peppe stressed that it's just for a two-week visit. He only has Davide and his sister. Eventually Peppe plans to move to his parents' farm, and then Davide will live on one floor of the house next door and his sister will live on the other. The point is that they'll all live in Supino."

"Maybe Peppe would like to visit Toronto?"

"Peppe won't fly."

I repeated this conversation to Kathryn. I said that Italians don't share the North American idea that you can choose individuality over what's best for the family. Personal desires are not important. It's all about accepting responsibility and remaining true to the family.

She said, "I know."

The house in the piazza was still for sale and I was still unsure. I'd had a few freelance pieces published in the *Toronto Star* and I was thinking of pitching my editor the idea of postcards from a small Italian village. The stories could be published weekly in the newspaper and I could write them during a six-month stay in Supino.

"Should we make an offer on the place?" said Bob.

"Not yet," said Joe. "I told the German guy that no one wants a house with three rooms on three levels. I get a better price next year. What do you think about putting a few tables and chairs in front?"

"I was thinking about that. Would we need to get a permit?"

"I get the permit to sell drinks. What about the coffee?"

"I was thinking of buying a coffee roaster. I can get a

small one shipped down from Milan. That way I could roast a few pounds every morning. What do you think, Joe?"

"I gotta get a permit for that. Like the peanut roaster or the chestnut roaster. Won't cost too much."

"But do you think it's a good idea? I want to make the bar a little different."

"Sure, it's good. Where you going to get the green coffee beans? Africa?"

"No, I'll buy through my green-bean importer. Some Brazilian, some Colombian."

"Maybe we get the donkey to bring the beans up to the piazza each morning," said Joe. "What do you think?"

Seven

For the past couple of years, I'd been writing stories about my father's village and our trip back to Supino with him. I wasn't sure whether anyone outside of our family would be interested in our experience, but I had an agent and she was trying to find a publisher. She phoned me in Toronto on an August evening when Bob was going to the corner store to buy a newspaper and I was about to kiss him goodbye at the door. My agent said, "Your book's been picked up by a publisher here on the West Coast. Their editor will be in touch with you next week." I grabbed Bob's hands and we jumped up and down in the kitchen like a couple of kids.

"I want to phone everyone I know and tell them the news," I said.

"Go ahead," said Bob. "I'll be back in a few minutes." And he went off to buy the newspaper.

I picked up the phone. I talked to people, I left messages,

and I didn't get tired of repeating the news. I phoned a friend who was on holiday in Sweden and the phone rang and rang before someone answered. I'd forgotten about the time difference and had woken my friend as well as the family she was staying with, but we didn't care. We were that happy. Bob returned with the newspaper and a box of chocolate-covered maraschino cherries.

It took a few days for the news to really settle in and eventually I ran out of people to tell. I started telling strangers: the man who fixed my computer, the clerk at the post office, the waitress, and the dry cleaner. The contracts arrived, but I was too excited to concentrate. Bob read them for me. Then I picked a time when Bob and Kathryn and I were all at the coffee company and I called my agent on one line and my brother and sister on the other lines so we could all be together while I signed the contract. Afterwards we went out for dinner and sat on the patio of our favourite restaurant, eating pizza, drinking wine, and pretending we were in Supino.

We were unwrapping those little candies they give you at the end of your meal along with your bill when Kathryn said, "Dad, I think that bump on your cheek is getting bigger. Maybe you should have the doctor take a look at it."

Bob never went to the doctor because he was never sick. He agreed it was important to have annual physicals, but he never found the time. He wouldn't have found the time to make an appointment for this either, so I made it for him. Our family doctor agreed with Bob, he didn't think it was anything, a lump that had always been there. Still, he sent Bob to a specialist and the specialist was stumped too and made an appointment for Bob to see another specialist downtown. Bob, who rarely complained, began to grumble about the amount of time he spent waiting in doctors' offices for nothing.

"Okay," I said, "just keep this last appointment and then we'll forget about it."

He came home so late that night that we'd already eaten dinner. I pulled his aluminum-foil-covered plate from the oven and we sat at the table. The kitchen curtain was still open because I'd been watching for his car in the driveway and the sky was black. No stars, no moonlight. The night looked more like a gloomy January evening than an evening in early autumn, and Bob looked tired.

"Traffic was heavy," he said.

"What'd the doctor say?" I asked.

Bob moved his eyes toward Kathryn. "How was class today?" he asked.

"Good. What'd the doctor say?" said Kathryn.

"It's just like I said. Nothing. They're going to take a sample of fluid from the lump and send it to the lab. Did you buy your university parking pass today?"

"When are they taking the sample?" said Kathryn.

"No hurry," said Bob. "Next month."

Bob was sitting on the edge of the bed when he told me the rest of the story. The doctor had tried to take the fluid sample in the office. He had a long needle and said Bob would only feel a quick prick before he drew out the liquid. "He tried to prick the lump and couldn't," Bob said. "He jabbed again and I honestly thought I was going to pass out. That's when he decided I needed to see a different specialist.

I said, 'What if I do nothing? Just leave well enough alone?' The doctor said he didn't recommend it."

"What *is* he recommending?"

"A biopsy."

The specialist's secretary called the next day with the booking. She said it was a day surgery and Bob would be in and out in a few hours. The specialist would remove the lump and take a look at it under the microscope. I wrote all of this down and passed Bob the note when he got home.

"Don't tell the kids," he said. "I don't want them to worry."

"*I'm* worried."

"It's nothing."

The surgery was booked for the morning of the third Thursday in November. I decided not to think of it as surgery, instead pretending the procedure was just a way to make the patient more comfortable while the doctor cut out some tissue for testing. Like freezing a patient's mouth when a dentist removes a tooth. I sat at the hospital with Bob, waiting for the call to the surgical unit. I kept getting up to pace a little before returning to the plastic chairs. Bob was playing with his wedding band, twisting it around and around.

"I'm sure you're right," I said. "It'll turn out to be nothing."

"I've been asking myself, 'What's the worst they can say?' I don't want to wake up and hear the doctor say, 'It's cancer.'"

"You won't."

And I was right. While Bob was in post-op, the surgeon had come out still dressed in his scrubs to give me the diagnosis, and then he was back in surgery, operating on the next patient, and *I* was the one who'd have to say it. I was sitting beside Bob when he woke up. He smiled when he opened his eyes and saw me. "I don't have anything on under this gown, you know," he said, grinning.

"It's cancer," I told him.

He closed his eyes. "I'm going to go back to sleep for a while."

I went down the hall to the waiting room and phoned my brother. "I'm at the hospital with Bob. No, nothing's wrong. It's just that he had a lump removed from his cheek and it turns out it's cancer. He didn't want anyone to worry. They don't know. Might be oral cancer or throat cancer or tongue cancer. No, there's no point. By the time you got here, we'd be checking out to go home. Yes, I'll be careful driving. Yes, I'm going to call him right now."

Our son Ken was living in Ohio, and when I called I got the answering machine. It didn't seem like the kind of message you should leave on a machine but I did. Then half an hour later I called again. And again, saying I'd call one more time at 5 p.m. and after that he could call me at home.

At five o'clock, as I walked back to the bank of telephones to make the final call, I had the idea that if I called from a different telephone, Ken would answer. I told him this when he picked up. "Yes, it does sound a little crazy," I admitted. "No, I think I'm okay. He's still sleeping. He didn't want you to worry. They aren't sure what kind of cancer. The incision's nothing. He's just groggy. We come back in two days. Then we'll know what we're dealing with. Yes, I'll tell him. Yes, I'll drive carefully. Yes, I'll phone when I get home."

When I got back to the room, Bob was awake and the doctor was just finishing his examination. "The nurse will give you the appointment information," the doctor said.

"Let's get out of here," said Bob.

By the time I'd picked up the information from the nursing station, Bob was dressed and waiting in the hallway. "Do you want to wait in the lobby while I get the car?" I asked.

"Why? I'm fine. Let's stop for dinner before we go home. I'm starving, and there's a new place on Dundas I want to try."

I didn't tell him that I was so scared I couldn't eat.

We went to a friend's birthday party that weekend. Our friend Joy, who was a retired nurse, noticed the small scar on Bob's cheek and asked him about it.

"They removed a little lump," said Bob.

"Any follow-up?" Joy said.

"I'm going back next week. This is a nice house. I like the log construction."

"Yes," agreed Joy. "We want it to have all our favourite things since this is the house where we're going to grow old together."

I stepped outside with that phrase pounding in my chest: would Bob and I grow old together?

Joy was beside me in a moment. "What's really going on?" she said.

I told her what we knew so far.

"If you ask the doctors for a straightforward assessment,

including his chances, they'll give you an honest answer," Joy said. "If you want to know."

"Of course I want to know."

"Not everyone does. Sometimes it's easier to handle things as they happen rather than face it all at once."

"No, I can deal with it. I just need to know what we're dealing with."

"How's Bob handling it?"

"He's not making it the centre of his life."

"Are you going to Italy soon?"

"We just got back a few months ago. I guess we'll go again in the spring, or the summer. It depends."

"Go to Supino. It's always good for you."

A letter arrived from my editor introducing herself and laying out the schedule for the publication of my book. Since the publisher was on the West Coast, we'd work together via telephone, computer, and mail.

I called my agent. "I'm not sure I can do this," I said. "Bob has cancer and we don't know yet if he'll need surgery."

"Do you want me to try to get a later publication date?"

"Would they go for that?"

"Yes, but they wouldn't guarantee that they'd publish you at the later date. It all depends on how many other books they have on their list. It's a bit of a gamble."

"I just want the book to be as good as it can be and I don't know if I can concentrate."

"What does Bob say?"

I hadn't asked him, not wanting to burden him with

mundane things. I explained it all to him that evening. "What are the chances of a first-time author getting published?" asked Bob. I'd already told him this number months ago: 2,000 to one. I wrote back to the editor and asked her to send the first edits whenever she was ready.

The next week, we were downtown at the Wharton Head and Neck Centre at the Princess Margaret Hospital for our appointment with the specialist. The waiting room was large and crowded; we found seats near the window where Bob pretended to read a magazine and I stared out the window at nothing. I'd spent a fair amount of time waiting in doctors' offices when our children were young and I was never very good at waiting, but now that Bob was the patient, I became calm. I knew he was worried and I didn't want to add to it with my own nervousness. So, as I stared out the window, I thought of all the Italian words that meant tranquility — *placida, serena, tranquilla, pace* — and hoped they would seep through my body and I'd become the words.

"Peppe told me a story about when he was a boy," said Bob. "Every morning, around one or two o'clock, the men and donkeys would gather at that little piazza to go up the mountain to cut firewood. Later the women met at the same piazza. They'd have copper pots to carry the water; most of them balanced the jugs on their heads. The women also carried baskets packed with their men's lunches. On their way back, they'd fill their empty baskets with twigs for the fire. The part that Peppe really liked was that as the women set out, they began singing and you could hear their voices growing softer as they climbed higher. Now Peppe says the villagers have indoor plumbing so there's no need to gather and walk singing to the mountain. It sounded better in Italian, but he said something like, 'The women are rich because of the indoor plumbing, but they're poor because they've lost the singing and the camaraderie.' Peppe said that if you want to see those copper pots now, you have to go to the souvenir shop. They're called *congono* in Supinese."

"I wish I could add that little story to the book," I said.

"I wish we were in Supino," said Bob.

"The only thing we know for sure," said the specialist, when we'd been called into his office, "is that nothing will be decided today. There's no urgency. We want to be sure of our diagnosis before we do anything."

We'd sat for over an hour in that crowded waiting room and Bob had been agitated the whole time. Now when the doctor used the words *no urgency*, I could feel Bob relax. The doctor asked if we'd mind if he called in his colleague from down the hall. Bob said, "Why not? We're already here."

Bob's x-rays were up on the screen and several specialists took a look and offered different explanations, but the one I remember was the doctor who compared cancer to the roots of a tree. He said, "The lump that we removed is like the tree trunk, but, just like a tree, cancer sends out its roots below the skin. We can't just dig a hole and pull out the roots. Some will break off. We have to make sure we get them all and the area around them so there's no cancer left to multiply and send out new shoots."

There was a little conference between the doctors and talk of rearranging schedules. I stared at the x-ray and wondered where those cancer roots had travelled. Bob checked his watch. "It won't be much longer," I said. "Once we know what we're dealing with, it'll be fine. I'm going to write down everything they say. It'll be fine."

"It's cancer of the parotid gland," began the oncologist. "That's a gland just in front of your ear that secretes saliva. The problem with it is that it's connected to a whole bunch of other areas, so a tumour like yours is difficult to pinpoint, especially if it has an extensive root system, which your tumour has. Most are benign, yours isn't . . . stage 3 . . . fast-growing . . . rare adenocarcinoma . . . less favourable prognosis . . . extensive surgery followed by aggressive radiation . . ."

I stopped writing and took Bob's hand. He was staring at the x-ray. I wasn't sure if he was listening anymore.

"We work on a priority basis so that the more urgent cases are done first," said the oncologist. "For example, a woman was in here earlier with a small scaly patch on her arm. We'll get to her in a few months. She's not urgent, not going to die in the next few months . . ."

Bob said, "When can you do the surgery?"

"The nurse will let you know. It'll be high priority, and we'll move you up if there's a cancellation."

"Who'd cancel surgery?" I asked Bob when we were back in the waiting room.

"Death," he said.

I called my cousin Bill late that night, after Bob was asleep. My cousin was asleep too, but he answered. I told him what the oncologist had said, repeating word for word, "A woman was in here earlier with a small scaly patch on her arm. We'll get to her in a few months. She's not urgent, not going to die in the next few months . . ."

Bill said he didn't think Bob was going to die in the next few months either. "They'll do the operation and he'll be okay."

"But, what if?"

"You'll cope," said Bill.

So we decided that night that Bob had enough to worry about and I wouldn't burden him with my fears. I'd cope. And if I thought that I couldn't, I'd call Bill.

While we waited for the surgery date, we tried to carry on with our usual activities. Bob was determined that the cancer would not be the centre of his life — his centre would be his family and his community, as always. I did a lot of research, feeling I could handle anything as long as I knew what we were in for. I wanted to follow Bob's lead and continue with our lives, but sometimes, in the night, I'd wake in a sweat thinking Bob had died. I'd open my eyes to reassure myself that Bob was right there beside me like always. Outside the window, the night sky was as dark as my thoughts. I couldn't fathom the idea of a life without Bob, a man I'd known since I was 17 years old and he gave me a ride home from the library in his Chevy II convertible and my life had changed in an instant.

Bob carried on with the Supino Social Club activities, planning the Christmas party and discussing the pros and cons of holding the polenta feast outdoors in January like they did in Supino.

"We'd just need to get a few things," said Bob. "Some giant cooking pots and wooden oars for stirring."

"Where are you going to hold it?" I asked. In Supino, this winter *festa* was held on the piazza in front of the Church of San Nicola. The cooking pots were set over open fires on the cobblestones.

"That's the problem. The City of Toronto requires permits and they don't allow outdoor fires. We told the clerk that we're not burning leaves, just making a fire to cook polenta, but he said, 'What's polenta?'"

"Well, you've got time. It's only October."

"If we were in Supino," began Bob, "I'd be able to help Peppe with his chestnut harvest. He has these wooden rakes hanging up in his shed at his farm. You whack the chestnuts with them to break the skin. You have to wear gloves because of the prickly shell . . ."

That winter a lot of Bob's conversations would begin with "If we were in Supino . . ." and most of mine would begin with "What if . . . ?" But I kept those conversations to myself.

Bob's surgery was scheduled for January. Then it was moved up twice. Every time the doctors spoke to us, they added more information.

"This is more complex than heart surgery, so you can expect an 11- or 12-hour operation."

"There'll be an incision from the top of his ear down his cheek, his neck, into his shoulder. A second incision under his neck."

"After we remove all the cancer, his face will be sunken. The muscle will grow back in a year or so. Unless the cancer comes back."

"Radiation every weekday for seven weeks. Burning the throat like that makes swallowing difficult. He won't be able to eat. He'll have to be on a liquid diet. If it gets too bad, we'll hospitalize him and put him on an IV. We'll have to remove his salivary glands, so he'll need to carry a bottle of water everywhere he goes."

Every weekend in November, Bob combed through his photos from Supino and put them into albums. It took a long time because he'd often pause to say, "Remember this?" Bob and my father sitting at the kitchen table, eating watermelon and spitting the seeds out the back door into the ravine; Bob and my father on the balcony hanging a clothesline; Kathryn and me sitting on the front steps writing postcards; Kathryn and Davide on the motorcycle; Angela in her kitchen window; Benito with plants in hand; Joe at our front door with a basket of eggs, with a jug of wine, with a bowl of figs; Peppe with a basket of hazelnuts from the mountain; Joe and Bob and Benito hanging decorations for the Feast of San Lorenzo.

Who was the saint that people prayed to for good health?

My book edits arrived. I started reading the suggestions and after a few minutes, I put the pages down.

"I don't think I can do it," I said. "It's too many things to consider. There are hundreds of pages and corrections on every one."

"One page at a time," said Bob.

"Look at this page, for example. She suggests moving this paragraph, cutting this whole line and she wants to know the relationship between us and the cousins who live on the farm."

"Okay," said Bob. "So one paragraph at a time."

An envelope came from Peppe. Inside were two photographs of Supino taken from high up on the mountain and showing the village laid out below, all terra cotta roofs and winding streets. Bob got out the magnifying glass. When he found our house, he used the expression that my father had always used: "She looks good." I was glad we'd spent the extra money to have our roof retiled with authentic terra cotta tiles instead of the new plastic ones that were starting to show up on rooftops here and there in Supino. The terra cotta tiles aged beautifully, their colours fading through the decades. When we climbed up the streets of old Supino Centro, where the houses dated back hundred of years, we could stop and look down on the wonderful patchwork of rooftops.

One time when we were walking the winding streets, Bob said, "Did you ever consider that we might have ended up buying a house in this old part of town?" We'd bought our house, sight unseen, with only a description from my cousin Johnny saying that he'd been in the house once and it had three rooms, a fireplace, and was located just up from the water fountain. A lot of houses were crammed into the streets just up from the water fountain.

"We could have bought one of these places," said Bob, looking at the houses that hugged the mountainside, the flat roof of one house doubling as a patio for the one above.

Some houses had a wide windowsill or doorway where the owner kept potted plants or a motor scooter. There were serpentine paths chiselled between the rocks. Narrow steps ran parallel to the houses. Every available recess was filled with a dwelling: one room, two rooms, and, if you were fortunate, a third room perched above. A recess too small for a house might contain a garden, a clothesline, and a wooden chair. If we'd bought here, we'd have had to park at the piazza centrale and carry everything up the winding pathways.

"Imagine bringing in the furniture or even the firewood," said Bob. "Thank goodness for Camillo."

"Who's Camillo?"

"The donkey who carries the supplies."

"How do you know his name?"

"You know," said Bob, using that circular Supinese hand motion.

The surgery was now scheduled for the second week in December: Bob would be home for Christmas and able to start radiation in the new year. Our son Ken had come up from Ohio to help out at the coffee company and Kathryn had taken a leave from her university classes. They said they'd take care of the business and I could take care of Bob and the book edits. We all said that everything would be fine.

The day before the surgery, the doctor said, "Don't come to the hospital and sit in the waiting room all day. It's a 12-hour operation. Come later, around five."

We were in the waiting room by nine. There were a few

other groups. Toward 11 o'clock, a woman approached the waiting-room volunteer to complain. "The doctors said they'd be done by 10:30 and they'd come out and tell us how things went. It's almost 11. What's going on?"

The volunteer tried to calm the woman by explaining that surgery can begin a little late, there can be small complications, that the doctor would be out as soon as possible, and the woman needed to stay calm.

"Complications?" said the woman. "Late? Calm? You try staying calm when your father's in surgery. They said 10:30 and . . ."

The volunteer had to call security. Security had to take the woman outside.

I said to my children, "We're not going to behave like that."

At noon we were discussing lunch, but no one wanted to leave. Ken finally said, "I'll go and pick up some sandwiches. Nothing's going to happen during the next half hour." As soon as Ken left, the doctor arrived. It was too early for news. Only four hours had passed. They'd said 11 or 12 hours. It had to be bad news. Had the cancer spread so far they couldn't remove it?

"The surgery's going well," the doctor said. "My colleague has taken over the next shift and I'll be back in at four. We need you to sign permission for us to graft a vein from Bob's leg in case we need to remove the vein near his eye."

I explained it all to Ken when he returned with lunch.

"Remove the vein near his eye?" said Ken.

"I know," I said, but I didn't. I'd heard the doctor, but I hadn't envisioned the wait and I hadn't visualized how Bob would look afterwards. At five o'clock, the volunteer said the waiting room was closing.

"But my husband's still in surgery," I said. "You can't close. Where are we going to go?"

"There's a waiting room on the fourth floor, at the end of the intensive care unit. You can wait there. Your husband will be in recovery for a while before they move him to step-down."

"What's step-down?"

"The area between intensive care and a regular room."

I thought of it as limbo, someplace between heaven and hell where people lingered while their fate was decided. We went to the new waiting room. It was heading to nine o'clock and we were watching the elevator every time the bell rang, hoping it was a stretcher and hoping Bob was on it.

A stretcher arrived. An old man with a thin face sat up on one elbow and looked around anxiously. As soon as he saw me, his face relaxed, he smiled a big lopsided smile, and I realized it was Bob. The incision was terribly long and held together with dozens of giant silver staples; the left side of Bob's face was deflated as if his cheek had caved in and the deflation continued right down his neck and into his left shoulder. He lifted his right arm and waved.

Bob was home for Christmas and back at the hospital every weekday in January for radiation. We missed the Supino Social Club polenta festival. "Next year," I said. "By then they'll have an outdoor permit."

A cardboard tube arrived in our mailbox. Inside was a

note from Joe: "Your cousin told me you had an operation, Bob. Get better soon and come back to Supino." And
a charcoal sketch of the polenta pots set up over open fires
in front of the Church of San Nicola.

"Let's frame it," I said. "We can hang it in the dining
room."

"Next year, I want to be there," said Bob. "Joe said he'd
get me on the committee of men who stir the polenta pots."

"You don't even like polenta."

"But I like the sausages that they serve with the polenta."

I'd heard the word *radiation* without ever thinking about what
it actually was. In Bob's case, it meant that the radiologist
would burn Bob's throat five times a week and Bob would
have a permanent sore throat. "Like strep throat that never
gets better," said the doctor. "Until the radiation ends in
seven weeks."

Bob and I went to the first treatment together, but after
that he said he'd drive himself. I wanted to set up a schedule
for people eager to help and let our friends and family take
turns driving Bob to his radiation appointments.

"It will give people a chance to spend some time with
you," I said.

"That's not how I want to spend time with people," said
Bob.

So Bob drove himself, fitting the radiation appointments into his daily schedule as if they were just another
entry on the day's to-do list. During those seven weeks he
stopped in to visit existing coffee customers, set up new

ones, and kept his radiation appointments at Princess Margaret Hospital. He stopped at the gift shop on the way out, only now, instead of buying himself a chocolate bar, he bought a bottle of water.

The weekends were a little easier because there were two days without radiation. We were on the same seven-week deadline: I had to finish the edits and he had to finish the radiation. Often on a Sunday afternoon, I'd read parts of the book to Bob, and sometimes, when I looked up, he'd be fast asleep. Soon he couldn't swallow anything but liquid, and then even liquids were too painful. He lost 30 pounds. At the end of the sixth week, we hosted a little birthday cel-ebration for Bob's dad, and Bob's throat was so sore he couldn't swallow the cake or the ice cream. As his parents were leaving, his father commented that there was only one more week of radiation, and Bob said, "I can't do it anymore."

His father said, "You have to do it. What's the alternative?"

Bob finished the radiation in March, one week before the wedding celebration for the daughter of one of the Supino Social Club executives.

The day that we dressed for the wedding, I noticed that his shirt was too big around the neck. When Bob tightened his tie, the tie puckered his shirt collar. We had to put two new holes in his good leather belt. When Bob put on his jacket, it looked like he'd borrowed someone else's suit.

"I look like some sort of clown," said Bob.

"You look great," I said.

"Great if I was impersonating a scarecrow," said Bob.

After the wedding ceremony, outside the church, people

offered their congratulations to the bride and groom and then they came to shake hands with Bob. That was the first day that Bob was able to swallow his food and he ate course after course and still lined up with the other guests to tackle the midnight dessert buffet.

Bob went for his follow-up oncology appointment and the prognosis was good. The second one was even better. He regained the lost weight. He did his exercises to rebuild the muscles in his left arm and shoulder. We got used to his sunken cheek and shrivelled neck and sloping shoulder.

Davide came to Toronto that summer for a two-week visit. As soon as he arrived, he telephoned his father. I heard him assure Peppe that Bob was well. After that first day, we saw very little of him. He and Kathryn would take off after breakfast and be gone for most of the day. They went to the museum and the art gallery and Kensington Market and Queen Street West and the Harley-Davidson motor-cycle shop and the movies. He called home to Supino on Sundays to speak to his father and sister. It was raining the day Kathryn took him back to the airport.

My Father Came from Italy was launched in October, so instead of helping Peppe with his chestnut harvest, Bob was sitting in the front row and I was reading from my book. Members from the Toronto Supino Social Club came to the event at the Columbus Centre; the women brought baskets of homemade biscuits and cookies. I found out there were Supino Social Clubs in Montreal, Vancouver, Ottawa, and Sudbury; they all invited me to come and read from my book. Every reading and signing through the fall and winter, Bob was in the front row. In the spring, the book was published in the States, where there were even more Supino Social Clubs, and my American publicist set up a book tour for September starting in New York. We booked a trip to Supino for July and August. I packed a few copies of the book in my suitcase.

Bob went to his last doctor's appointment the same week we left for Supino. "I don't have to go back for three months," he reported. "And after that appointment, six months, and then I don't have to go back for a year."

Eight

Usually we arrived in the village in the mid-afternoon, but that July we had a series of delays at the airport and the car rental, and we'd stopped to eat at the auto grill. The sun was dropping toward Santa Serena, sending shadows down the street, when we finally arrived in the village. As we drove up the main street, I checked my watch. It was barely six o'clock.

"Why are all these stores closed?"

"Festa?"

"I don't think so. The Kennedy Bar was open, but the greengrocer's closed and the wool shop. Wait a minute, wasn't there a little gift store there beside the barber?"

We stopped at the red light on the hill. The windows of the hardware store were papered with yellowed newspapers. Next door, the shoe store's window was empty except for a sign that said, "For Lease."

As we drove through the tunnel and up the hill toward

our street, we saw that the pizza store was open but the greengrocer that used to be there was gone.

Bob slowed down to wave to Benito, who was sitting on the bench with some friends, and Benito motioned for us to stop. The men came to the car window to shake Bob's hand. They hid their surprise when they saw Bob's sunken face, and patted his shoulder. "Welcome back," they said. "Welcome home."

A truck pulled up behind us and beeped; Cristina from the *tabacchi* store came out and waved the vehicle past. Then she and her customer came to shake Bob's hand. Alfredo and Carlo, the mechanic, walked down the street to see what was going on. A few minutes and a few more handshakes passed before we were able to drive up our street. Mario's rosemary hedge had grown so fat that I had to close my window before Bob pulled the car up tight against the fence. When we got to the house, Peppe was waiting by his front door. He said, "Hello, Bob. I speak English. How are you, my friend?"

"You speak English!" said Bob.

"I speak English. How are you, my friend?" repeated Peppe.

"Bene," said Bob. *"Molto bene."*

Peppe had helped Bob to unload the suitcases from the trunk onto the roadway and now he lifted one to carry to the house, but Bob took the case. *"Posso,"* Bob said. *I can do it.*

"Okay," said Peppe, using the last of his English words. He waited until Bob was climbing the stairs before he asked me, "Bob okay?"

Now it was my turn to use the Italian words I'd memorized in anticipation of the neighbours' questions about

Bob's face, starting with the word *cancer*. I said that the operation was successful and the radiation should prevent the
cancer from returning, and the doctors could even recon-
struct his face next year with surgery, if Bob wanted.

"Basta," said Peppe, shaking his head. That had been Bob's
reaction as well. He'd had enough surgery. But I'd noticed
that Bob avoided having his photo taken now and he'd told
me that he'd taught himself to shave without looking in
the mirror, so I thought he might change his mind on the
reconstruction.

By now Joe had come out of his garage to shake Bob's
hand.

"Today's the festival for grandparents," said Joe. "There's
a troupe of street performers from Rome coming. I'm going
down to decorate a little bit." He had a roll of plastic flags
under his arm. "You coming?" he asked, pointing to the
water fountain just down the street from our house.

"Let me get the rest of this stuff inside first," said Bob.

As usual, Angela had rearranged our furniture after
she'd cleaned our house. This time the kitchen table and
chairs were in the living room under the disco light and the
chesterfield was in the kitchen, pushed up in front of the
patio door. I took down the calendar that Angela had hung
above the fireplace. It had a photo of a suburban mall with
an address in the next village.

"What the heck is Ferentino Mall?" I said.

"Just leave it," said Bob. "We can move the rest later."

We headed down to the corner. At the *tabacchi* store,
Cristina had opened her cantina doors. Inside, women were
making *prosciutto* and *porchetta* sandwiches, and stacking them

in pyramids on the table. Joe and Benito had a bar set up beside the water fountain where they were pouring wine for the adults and iced tea for the kids. "All free," said Joe.

Soon there was a crowd sitting in a circle of plastic lawn chairs, eating, drinking, and listening to the music coming from the speakers on someone's balcony. Many of the villagers came to shake Bob's hand. I thought some of these well-wishers were strangers, but Bob identified them all for me: the street sweeper, the butcher's brother visiting from Aliquippa, the man who owned the photography shop, the shepherd that he often met at the water fountain in the afternoons when I was sleeping and he was getting water, the woman who roasted the chickens down at the Kennedy Bar, the man from Rome who was renovating the highest house in Supino Centro, and the man in the grey fedora who owned the donkey, Camillo, who carried construction supplies up to that house.

Plastic flags fluttered in the breeze and there was a feeling of expectancy. We heard a drum as it echoed through the narrow street, the sound coming from near the Bar Italia. But instead of a drummer, a prince in a purple cape ran up the street. He swirled into the centre of the circle and, with a booming voice that matched the sound of the drum, began telling the crowd a story about a princess and a dragon. The children cheered when he mentioned the dragon. He lifted his sceptre and twirled it a few times. Flames burst out one end. The prince swallowed the flames and held out his fiery sceptre to the crowd.

"Anyone want to swallow fire?"

"I'm going to call it a night," said Bob. "You stay if you want."

"Are you all right?"

"Just tired," he said.

Bob left my side, and a moment later I saw Kathryn and Davide work their way through the crowd.

"Is Dad all right?"

"Just tired from the flight."

"Do you think the fire-eater reminded him of the radiation?"

"Let's give him a few minutes, then I'll go up and see."

By the time I got to the house, Bob was already asleep. He hadn't even taken the time to move the bed to the window so we could sleep beneath the stars. I opened the window to the Big and Little Dippers, which were outlined clearly in the dark Supino sky. The moon, barely half full, shone its pale light onto the bed. Bob was sleeping in his usual position, his left arm extended and his left cheek resting on his shoulder. I slipped in behind him and put my arm around his waist.

"Mmm," I said.

"Mmm," he said.

That was our signal that everything was okay.

The next morning I was coming down the stairs just as Bob was pulling the chesterfield away from the back wall. He opened the kitchen door and said, "Our patio's been moved."

I looked outside. Our patio stones were missing, Benito's plants were missing, and the earth that once held our patio had been pushed about two metres beyond our back door.

An *X* made of two-by-fours blocked our exit. We stood behind the wooden barrier looking at nothing.

"Ey. I didn't know you come already. Welcome back," said our next-door neighbour Sam, who was standing in his backyard. "Come."

We walked out our front door, down the steps, past Sam's house, down his driveway and into his yard. Sam shook Bob's hand.

"What's going on?" said Bob, with a sweep of his arm to take in our missing patio.

"See here," said Sam, as he pulled a paper from his pocket. "Your property is 10 by 10. Ten years ago, I marked it on the wall in white paint, you remember, Bob? The measurements are here on the paper too. Some water was leaking into my back wall so I had to dig and waterproof the foundation. I figured I'd do yours at the same time. The tar covered the mark, so I repainted it. You want to measure? Make sure you still have your 10 feet?"

We certainly weren't going to measure and insult a neighbour who had just waterproofed our wall for us.

"Can I pay you?" asked Bob, even though we knew Sam would shake his head.

"One day my daughter will own my house just like Kathryn will have yours, so you have to take good care of the place. Will you have some coffee?"

We sat in Sam's yard and he told us the rest of his plans. First he was waiting for the tar to dry completely before he pushed the dirt back into place. "Probably tomorrow," he said. Then we'd have our yard again — that is, if tomorrow meant the next day and not sometime that summer. "Those

patio stones that Joe put for you were too old," he said.
"And I don't like terrazzo. I'll get the old tile-layer, Mario,
to lay authentic terra cotta tiles. Beautiful. Just like on your
roof. Authentic. Not like that plastic stuff people put today.
Then, I'll put the wrought-iron fence. We'll go together,
Bob, to the factory and pick what you like. You can pay for
the fence. What do you think Benito wants? Planter boxes
or iron frames to hold his pots of hanging flowers? I don't
like flowers myself. I grow zucchini, eggplant, tomatoes, all
organic. How long are you staying?"

"We're here until August 22," Bob said.

"Good. Welcome back."

We walked back to our house carrying a zucchini from
Sam's organic garden as well as a large bag of arugula.
"What's that?" I said, pointing to a narrow paper stuck
under our door.

"It looks like mail. Do you think it's our hydro bill?"

We raced up the stairs. Bob unfolded the paper. It was a
flyer advertising specials for the Ferentino Mall, the kind of
junk mail we always got in Toronto and had never seen in
Supino. Benito joined us and showed us his dustpan that
contained half a dozen flyers, some crumpled, some torn,
some with footprints on them. He shook his head.

"Benito doesn't like the flyers. They blow off the door
handles and clutter the street," said Angela from her
kitchen window. "A mall opened in Ferentino, like they
have in North America. Lots of stores inside and a big paved
parking lot. Only 20 minutes away. You can buy everything
you need in one trip."

I thought about the closed stores, the flyers littering

the streets. Another North American idea had come to Supino.

"What about the people who own stores in the village?" I said. "What about the greengrocer and the hardware store man and — ?"

"They go to the mall too," said Angela. "I can't talk now. I have a job."

"A job? Where?"

"City Hall. I clean the offices. That reminds me, Bob. The mayor's wife told me you didn't pay your water bill yet."

"What water bill?"

"The water bill you're supposed to pay every year."

"But where's the bill? Does it come to the house?"

"The man comes to your house and you pay him."

"When does he come?" I said.

"How much?" said Bob.

"I find out," said Angela.

Now that our patio issue seemed under control, and Angela was going to find out about our overdue water bill, Bob got the idea that we could solve the hydro issue. "I've asked Marco to call the office in Frosinone and make an appointment for tomorrow," he said. "Then we'll go together. We won't leave the office until we get the bill put into our names and sent to our house."

"Tomorrow's a civic holiday," Marco told us. "Civic workers will be on parade in Rome. But we have an appointment for the day after tomorrow at 9:30."

"We shouldn't have to wait long then," said Bob.

"Bring your passports, your fiscal code number from

Supino City Hall, and your ownership papers. Bring your business card too."

Marco drove, and we arrived in Frosinone with 10 minutes to spare, which he used trying to find a parking spot. Finally Marco pulled into the gas station across the street from the hydro building. He rolled down his window and had a quick conversation with the attendant. "Ten euro, please," Marco said to Bob. Bob handed the bills to Marco, who handed the money to the attendant. The attendant pocketed the money and gave a quick sideways nod toward a space with a sign that clearly said, "No Parking." That's where Marco parked the car.

The lobby of the hydro building was large and cool with white marble and ostentatious plants but no desks and no people. Marco led us to a side door and buzzed. I checked my watch; we were right on time for our 9:30 appointment. We walked into a room full of people. A machine was installed on the wall, like the kind they have at the deli counter where you take a number to be served. Marco took a number. "We have an appointment," I said.

"*Appuntamento*," said a woman who was sitting in a chair knitting. "Everybody has *un appuntamento*."

The door opened again and a man entered. He was carrying his lunch. I could smell the provolone cheese and peppers. He took a number. The sign said they were serving customer number 34; we were number 53.

"I can't sit here," said Bob. "I'll go for a walk and come back in an hour."

"Make it an hour and a half," said Marco.

We waited. People came in, and people went out, and we waited. The only break in the monotony came when the bell rang and the sign above the door changed to the next number. Number 44 flashed, but no one responded. The same thing happened with numbers 45, 46, and 47. The man who'd brought, and eaten, his lunch now folded his newspaper and began to watch the sign.

At 11:30, our number came up. I jumped out of my chair before the bell had finished its chime and hurried through the door into the inner office. There I saw two desks and two officials, both bored. I introduced myself in Italian, showed my Italian passport and my latest hydro bill. The official glanced at my papers, but he addressed Marco, "Fiscal code?"

Marco pointed to the number on the bill, but the official shook his head.

"I own the house," I said.

"Your name is not on the hydro bill, *signora*. Who pays the bill?"

"My travel agent. I send him the money and he pays."

"If he pays, he owns the house."

"I own the house."

"*Signora*, please, why would someone pay the bill if they didn't own the house?"

Out the window I could see our car parked at the gas station. I wondered about offering the official some cash. Bribing an official to send you a bill seemed wrong: I should be bribing him *not* to send us a bill.

"He's going to check with his superior," said Marco.

When the official returned, smelling strongly of coffee and cigarette smoke, he said, "The hydro will be turned on today at two o'clock. The bill will be sent to your address on *via condotto vecchio*, number 12."

I started to explain that we live at number 10 not 12, but Marco interrupted.

"Grazie. Arrivederci."

"But we're number 10," I said to Marco as we left the building.

"Maria, please. You'll have hydro this afternoon at two. What difference if the bill goes next door. Sam will stick it under your door. Where's Bob?"

We found Bob just crossing the street. He had a bunch of yellow gerber daisies in his hand. To celebrate our success with the hydro officials, we took Marco for lunch at the restaurant in the woods.

"This is my favourite restaurant," said Bob. "I'd like to eat lunch here every single day."

As usual, the owner, Guerrino, had the waiter bring us glasses of ice-cold limoncello to finish our meal.

"Do you really think we'll have hydro today?" I asked Marco.

"You worry too much, Maria. The official said today, therefore you'll have the hydro today."

And we did. But only because Marco and Joe ran the orange electrical cord across the road from their upstairs window to ours.

Guido came to the house that evening. He shook hands with Bob, then pulled his handkerchief from his pocket and wiped his eyes. "Bob, my Canadian brother," he said. "You're too skinny. Come to my house for lunch on Sunday."

Joe knocked on the door a few minutes later with biscotti

that Angela had made. Bob poured glasses of vermouth, and Guido opened the back door.

"Don't go out," said Joe. "The cement's not dry."

"What cement?" I said. "Sam said terra cotta tiles, not cement."

"Maria," said Joe, "I told you this before. You worry too much. The cement is not for *you* to sit on. The *tiles* will sit on the cement."

"You're putting new tiles?" said Guido.

"No. Sam is putting the tiles in exchange for the soil beneath the patio."

"The soil belongs to you."

"But we don't need the soil and we do need new patio tiles. Sam is going to build a cantina under the patio."

"Under *your* patio?" asked Guido.

"I've been thinking about it," said Joe, holding his glass out for a refill. "If you keep the soil, you can grow things."

"I'd rather have a patio than a garden."

"*Mamma mia!*" said Guido. "I can plant a few things for you: lettuce, onions, tomatoes, peppers, zucchini, some swiss chard. I'll build a little chicken coop on the side of the garden too and Bob can eat fresh eggs every day."

"What are we going to do with a chicken when we go home next month?"

"Roast it, no?"

The next thing I knew the men were in the backyard, talking loudly. Guido seemed to be marking out the proposed chicken coop, but Bob was shaking his head. Then Sam was showing them the future cantina, stepping back to demonstrate how the doors would open into his yard, and Guido was shaking his head. The conversation accelerated. I gave up trying to translate. The men waved to me as they went on their way.

"See you on Sunday," said Guido.

Bob came into the house and said, "It's the old good news—bad news scenario. The good news is that Sam's going to build you a pizza oven."

"Yeah," I said, "I've always wanted a pizza oven. Wait a minute. Where's he building it?"

"That's the sort of bad news," said Bob. "He's building it in his backyard."

"*Mamma mia*. Just once, I'd like to have one thing go the way that I want it. I know they live here and we're just summer visitors, I know they mean well and they're looking out for us and all that stuff, but really, Bob, look at those darned ceramic tiles behind the sink — they're the ugliest thing I've ever seen next to this crazy disco light. We can't even keep our furniture the way we want it — we have to sneak around moving our bed under the window and every single time we come I have to search for that blue ceramic plate with the sunflower and hang it back up above the fireplace and take down the latest calendar or picture of San Cataldo or photo of the Lazio soccer team that Angela has hung there. And what's that wardrobe doing in our bedroom and how on earth did Joe get it up the stairs and did you notice that it's blocking the fold-down ladder that leads to the attic? How are we supposed to get up there? And another thing, every time we come, our patio is moved or missing or being replaced or — I don't even know why I'm saying *our* patio because it's like everyone but us makes the decisions and I would just like one thing to go my way. Just one."

"I said no to the chickens," said Bob. "Sam said you can use the pizza oven anytime you like. Joe's going to stack some small logs just for the oven. I think he's planning to use it too. Tonight I'll take you to the restaurant in the woods and we'll sit on the terra cotta tiles and admire the garden and eat pizza and pretend the patio and the garden are all ours."

I thought about Bob's idea to open a coffee bar in the village. I thought about dealing with the hydro officials and the neighbours and the laws of Supino — if they really were laws — but I didn't say anything to Bob. For him, it was more than opening a business; it was an Italian adventure. Why dampen his dreams with my reservations? For Bob, it was all about becoming Italian.

On the way to the restaurant, we stopped at the piazza at San Pietro, because I wanted to look up an address. Somewhere on the street that ran from the church down to the main street was a house where a man named Sergio Coletta had spent part of his childhood. Sergio now lived in Moss Point, Mississippi, and he had written me a letter, which had arrived on the same day we were packing for Supino. I'd tossed it into my suitcase. Sergio Coletta had written to say that he'd read a review of *My Father Came from Italy* in *USA Today* and he'd ordered the book online because the author's last name was the same as his. Imagine his surprise when he began reading the book and discovered that I was writing about Supino — the village where he was born. Sergio decided to write and tell me his story.

"I was born in Supino in 1929; my father died in 1933 and in 1935 my grandfather wanted my mother and me to come to America and live with him. My six years in Supino were centred around the Piazza del Popolo, *via Roma* 71, and the church of San Cataldo." Sergio went on to tell me about his Supinese relatives including his grandfather, "Giovanni, who had a dry goods and grocery store at the Piazza del Popolo."

Neither of those stores was there now and the church, which Sergio referred to as San Cataldo, was now known as San Pietro. He wrote that he knew very little about his father's side of the family, the Coletta side, except to say, "For reasons never explained to me there was 'bad blood' between the Tolfas and the Colettas. Probably one of those stupid hardheaded disagreements that can only happen in Italy, especially in a small village like Supino." His Coletta grandparents, Giovanni and Antonia Berrola Coletta, were unknown to me, but I was interested to read about his aunt, Maria Tolfa.

She taught school in Supino from 1923 to 1973. She retired as principal of the school at San Sebastiano, and died in 1997 at the age of 90. She was known as *Signorina Tolfa* or *Maestra Tolfa*. She lived at *via Roma* 71. She dedicated her life to seeing to it that the children of Supino received the best education possible. Many a farm family was talked out of ending their children's education after the sixth grade. She talked many other families into financing the children's education to become lawyers, accountants — professionals. There were over 400 Supinese in attendance at her funeral in April 1997.

It may have been the memory of his aunt who'd encouraged education for the Supinese children; it may have been the appeal of strong blue ink on thin airmail stationery; it may have been the simplicity of his sincere signature, *"Grazie, Sergio Coletta,"* but I felt the letter needed something more than just a standard acknowledgement for writing.

Bob parked the car at San Pietro and walked across the piazza to take some photos of the three-level house that was still for sale, and I walked down *via Roma* to number 71. Sergio's aunt had died four years earlier, but I couldn't tell if the house was inhabited or not. The forest-green door was covered with a thin layer of dust, but the planter beside it contained a small but healthy cedar shrub. There was a round doorknocker, but it too held a coating of dust. I looked around; all was quiet on *via Roma*. I sat on the front step and wrote:

> Dear Sergio, I am sitting on the steps of your aunt's house. In the distance I hear the bells of the goats that graze the hills behind the church and from below the voices of the men at the bar beside the Statue of the Fallen Soldier. Thank you for taking the time to write to me. I did not know about your grandfather's dry goods or grocery store that was once here. There are no shops surrounding the piazza now but there is a little house for sale, which my husband Bob wants to buy and open as a summer coffee bar . . .

When I finished the letter, I broke off a small branch from the cedar bush that grew beside the front door and enclosed it in the envelope. Probably you aren't allowed to send part of a plant from Supino to Moss Point, but I licked the envelope and decided not to think about such North American ideas.

Bob was leaning against the stone wall, enjoying the view of Supino's main street. He rested one foot on the wall, his camera slung over his right shoulder, and the sun was shining on his curly hair. If I avoided the left side of his face, Bob looked healthy. He turned when he heard my footsteps on the cobblestones and smiled his lopsided grin. "Ready?" he said.

Once we were seated at the restaurant in the woods, we discussed the purchase of the house in the piazza and the challenges of turning it into a summer bar. Bob was keen to bring in a small coffee roaster from Milan.

"Imagine the smell of the coffee beans roasting each morning. The breeze will carry the scent over most of the village. Who could resist that?"

"Will you sell by the pound?"

"At first, I thought, why not? But then, I thought the coffee should be tied to the café experience, you know? The villagers come to my bar for fresh-roasted espresso. Coffee never tastes the same at home — different water temperature or the portions aren't measured exactly or the grind's not consistent. If we can put some tables and chairs on the piazza, the summer tourists will have a great view of the sunsets behind Santa Serena. That's one of the advantages of this location — it's high. I'm not sure about the church though, they may not want us to be open when they're open for Mass. I have to ask Joe about it."

"What's Joe say about the idea of a patio?"

"He's working on it. Along with the permits. There seems to be some rule about how many bars there can be within a certain section of the village. Joe says they can't be too close to each other, which makes sense, but when I asked him about the Bar Italia and the bar without a name just down the street at the *piazza del l'erba*, he said that bar has been there a long time, before the rule. That bar actually has a name. It's La Vecchia Fontana — the old water fountain."

"That's perfect since there is no old water fountain, at least not that I've ever seen."

"Maybe there was one years ago. The *piazza del l'erba* doesn't contain a blade of grass, but maybe a hundred years ago it was flush with grass."

"What are you going to call your bar? Café San Pietro, for the church?"

"Café Coletta, for your father."

With those two words, Café Coletta, I put aside my worries about Bob's plans. I figured that if the bar didn't work out, we'd simply close it and rent out the house, or sell it. The important thing was for Bob to have the chance in the same way that we'd taken a chance on buying a house in the village.

The waiter brought our pizza on a metal pedestal.

"Do you remember?" I asked.

"I was just going to ask you the same thing," said Bob.

Years ago, when Bob took me home to meet his parents, they'd told me about going to Buffalo one Sunday for dinner. In my family, no one went out for dinner on a Sunday night, that was family night, and no one ever drove from Toronto to Buffalo for dinner, that would be a waste of gas. But Bob's family's not Italian. His parents were in this restaurant, just finishing their roast beef dinner, when the waiter passed by carrying a large plate in front of him.

"It was like a silver cake pedestal," Bob's mother said. They'd asked the waiter what he was serving — it smelled so delicious — and the waiter had said, "Pizza pie."

His parents were so intrigued with this new type of pie that they ordered one for dessert. "It tasted great," Bob's father said. "It's an Italian dish. Do you know it? Pizza pie."

Bob had grown up in a world completely different from mine. In the '60s, when we met, my parish priest was preaching that the more things a couple had in common, the better their chances were of making a successful marriage. I remember telling Bob about this the summer that we met, as he walked me home from the library. He pointed out an elderly couple coming toward us. They were well into their 70s; the man had a newspaper tucked under his arm, the woman carried a book, and they were talking softly to each other. Bob said, "That's how I want to be when I'm old, walking along enjoying the day and still holding hands with my wife."

We were married seven months later. Everyone said we were too young and our backgrounds were too different, but we'd seen our future in that older couple walking along holding hands. Now we would be that couple, walking along the cobblestone streets of Supino, for six months every year, and we'd still be holding hands.

The next morning we were heading out for coffee as Joe was driving out of his garage. He rolled down the car window.

"Ey, Bob, you come tonight?"

"Where?"

"The *festa*."

"What time?"

"About six."

"Where?"

"Usual place. See you later."

We passed the village priest, Don Antonio, who was en route to the water fountain.

"Welcome back." He shook Bob's hand. "Are you coming tonight? Good. You can carry the flag."

We asked Bianca at the Bar Italia what she'd heard about tonight's *festa*.

"Bob's carrying the flag, no?"

Angela was sitting at a table outside the bar, drinking cappuccino and chatting with Cristina.

"I thought you were working at the City Hall," I said.

"I'm on my break." It was barely 10 o'clock.

"Do you know anything about the *festa*?"

"It's a feast for the emigrants. First there's a mass at six o'clock at Maria Maggiore. Someone lays a wreath at the Statue of the Fallen Soldier. The band marches everyone down the street to the public garden —"

"What public garden?"

"Down the street. Bob, you carry the Canada flag. Someone from Detroit carries the American. Dinner at the *pensione* at Quattro Strade. No, this year it's at the new place, the Cowboy Restaurant."

"Are you coming, Angela?"

"I don't eat the hotta dog."

Nine

One of the very few — perhaps the only — event that starts on time in Supino is the daily six o'clock Mass at the Church of Santa Maria Maggiore. We arrived about 15 minutes early and the pews were already nearly filled. The altar was decorated with wildflowers from the mountain displayed in large copper pots. Some white satin bows with baby roses knotted into narrow ribbons were tied to the first half-dozen pews. *"Matrimonio,"* began the woman seated next to me, pointing to the bows, and then she continued in a torrent of Italian telling me all about yesterday's wedding. All I had to do was nod in agreement until there was a pause in the monologue.

"Were you there?" I asked in my best Italian.

"Oh, no," she said, and then she was off telling me the rest of the details of the wedding: the cost of the bride's dress, the courses served, the *bomboniere*, and then . . . the altar boys entered from the side altar and the Mass began.

My eye caught a patch of white dress shirt beneath a black Italian suit and the flash of a cufflink. A stranger tapped Bob on the shoulder and whispered, "Meet me outside after communion."

Bob nodded.

I whispered, "Who was that?"

Bob shrugged.

After the Mass, I hurried outside to the little piazza in front of the church and there was a crowd of band members, flag bearers, police officers, a man with a video camera, a photographer with his camera set up on a tripod atop his Fiat, and the usual assortment of villagers and stray dogs. The only thing missing was the ubiquitous traffic, but that was because the street was closed. Bob waved from behind the Canadian flag and before I could wave back, the man with the black suit and the flashy cufflinks raised his hand and — boom! — the band began their requisite marching song and the procession moved on down *via Regina Margherita*. The American and Canadian flags flanked the Italian flag, and behind them came an assortment of other banners and flags representing the region, the province, City Hall, and San Cataldo.

We marched to the bottom of the hill, where the procession met the lines of cars waiting for the street to reopen. Most of the cars were empty; I could see the drivers at the bar or just standing on the roadway, chatting.

The procession veered off to the left and up the stairs to the public garden, where I had yet to see a tree or a flower growing. There was a large cement pod almost the size of a tennis court, which was used during the summer months to host films under the stars. By the time I reached the top of the hill, the band had loosened their ties and tucked their hats beneath their elbows. The flags were lying lengthwise on the bleachers, and that popular refrain, "*Ci vediamo,*" see you later, was everywhere.

"That's it?" I said to Bob.

"That's it."

At the Cowboy Restaurant, the owner had set up the tables outside, so we didn't get the full effect of the saloon-like décor, complete with cowboy posters, that he'd created inside. However, speakers piped country music onto the patio area — Hank Williams was singing about a broken heart. Instead of the usual freshly pressed linen, the tables were covered with white paper held down in the corners by shiny tin horseshoes. In the centre of each table stood a silver serviette holder with paper napkins.

At the table next to ours some members of the Toronto Supino Social Club were talking to the mayor about renaming a street in the village "Toronto Street."

Someone from the Montreal Supino Social Club said, "Why Toronto Street? Why not Montreal Street?"

The discussion got a little louder with the mention of Vancouver Street and then a debate about which street might be appropriate for a name change. Everyone wanted a main street named after their North American city: no one wanted a side street or, even worse, a dead-end street.

Hank Williams was singing "Your Cheatin' Heart" when the antipasto arrived. Instead of the usual display of olives, cold cuts, cheese, and roasted peppers, there were wooden bowls of potato chips and pretzels and trays holding

old-fashioned glasses of Coke. The waiters put jars of mus-
tard, ketchup, and relish on each table. The guests started
to look around.

"Where's the cheese?" someone asked.

"No pasta tonight," said the owner. "It's American night
with American food. Hot dogs and hamburgers from the
grill."

The waiter put the first tray of hamburgers on the table.

"What's this?" said someone as he lifted the bun.

"It's a flat meatball."

"Where's the tomato sauce?"

"You put ketchup instead of tomato sauce."

The guests looked at each other. Someone broke off a
corner of a hamburger with his fork. *"Buono,"* he said. "A
little dry."

Someone passed the ketchup. The waiters brought
Budweiser beer and began pouring it into tall glasses. The
beer glasses had been engraved with *Festa dell'Emigrante*, and
the date. "A souvenir," said the waiters.

"Give me one," said the older woman sitting beside
me, and she opened her purse and tucked the glass inside.
Johnny Cash began strumming "Orange Blossom Special."
Beyond the twang of the guitar I could still hear the con-
versation about the renaming of streets — Windsor Street,
Sault Ste. Marie Street, Thorold Street, Hamilton Street,
Sudbury Street, and Aliquippa Street.

"That's an American city," someone said.

"So?"

One of the men left the table and walked over to ours
and introduced himself as a *paesano* from Pennsylvania. "My

name's Coletta like yours," said the American, as he pulled up a chair.

He was wearing Bermuda shorts and a T-shirt, so I knew he didn't live in Supino. Despite his American appearance, he had a warm and genuine Supinese familiarity that suggested that since our names were the same we were somehow related.

"I've been doing some research on my family tree and from what I can tell, there are four branches of the Coletta family in the village," he said. "I've never been able to go back far enough to connect them. I read your book, by the way. Enjoyed it a great deal."

Before I could respond, the stranger switched topics and continued, "Do you know Tchaikovsky's *Capriccio Italien*? Tchaikovsky composed it during his visit and tour of Italy in the 1880s. His melodies and themes are those that he heard in the various provinces. His main theme is from the area of Ferentino and Frosinone. My mother would always sing the lyrics whenever she heard this piece played on the radio. She told me that a man named Battisti owned a lot of land in the valley below Supino near the road leading to Ferentino. I understand your father's family farmed some of the Battisti land. My mother remembers as a young teenager how the women in the wheat field would sing this melody. One worker would start it and the others would all join in. The singing of the workers was something she always told me about. Tchaikovsky took this melody and made it the central theme of his *capriccio*. I have always regretted that I never asked her to write out the lyrics."

There was silence when the American Coletta finished

his story. After a moment, the woman with the beer glass in her purse began to hum a faint classical tune, but before others could join in there was a ruckus at the door of the western restaurant. "Yippee aye oh!" said the waiters as they pushed out the karaoke machine. "All you country music singers sign up for your turn to sing."

"Thank you for the lovely story," I said to the American. "My father used to talk about working those fields on the road to Ferentino."

"Have you been to the Ferentino Mall?" asked the American.

"It's not for me," I said. "I can do that kind of shopping at home. I prefer the outdoor markets."

"I guess we can't expect the village to stay the same forever."

"No."

But neither of us sounded convinced. Of course, one-stop shopping was simple and convenient for the villagers, but Supino had lost something with the opening of the mall. The villagers didn't have to bring their shopping baskets or canvas bags, because the mall stores provided plastic bags; the café in the mall served their espresso to go in small Styrofoam cups and the pizza restaurant was take-out only. The shoppers were hurried. In the village shops, the owners called everyone by name and the customers had time to chat. Often the shopkeeper's son or daughter would carry home the customer's purchases, packed in a cardboard box. At the mall, the customers pushed their purchases to their car in a shopping cart. Guido said that at the mall you don't even have to climb stairs, the stairs move for you. We stayed for the ice cream, served in glass dishes and topped with chocolate sauce and a maraschino cherry. When the waiters brought thin American-style coffee in thick white ceramic mugs, and Hostess cupcakes wrapped in cellophane, Bob pushed back his chair.

"Let's get going," he said.

Joe called over from the next table, "You leaving?" and when Bob nodded, Joe said he'd like a ride home.

"How did you like American night?" I asked.

"The beer was good," said Joe. "By the way, Bob, I was thinking we need to go back to the house in the piazza with Luigi."

"Who's Luigi?" I said.

"The plumber," said Bob. "I want to get a price on putting in a bathroom on the second floor. Then I can put together an offer for the owner."

"I told that German guy that no one wants to buy his house. If we wait for the spring, I'm pretty sure we'll get a better price."

"I think 50,000 euros is fair, Joe."

"The new bathroom's going to cost. Then the renovations for the bar. You have to buy the tables and chairs — I can get some used tables and chairs, Bob."

"No, everything's going to be new."

"Okay," said Joe, "whatever you want."

I gave my head a shake: Had Joe actually agreed to let Bob set up the bar his own way? Bob was smiling his lopsided grin as he reached for my hand. "Next year at this time, we'll be in business."

"Come in," said Joe when we arrived on *via condotto vecchio*. "Angela will make some spaghetti with olive oil and garlic."

"It's late," I said.

"Only takes a minute," said Joe. "And I'm hungry. What about you, Bob?"

"Starving," said Bob.

Before the church bells rang the half-hour, we were sitting at the table in Angela's kitchen. As she piled the spaghetti onto the plates, Joe grated the *parmigiano*. *"Buon appetito,"* he said, and he turned out the light. We ate our spaghetti by the light of the moon shining in the kitchen window.

Partway through the meal, I heard a whistle from the street below, and Angela got up and pressed the buzzer that opened the front door. "That's Benito," she said. "Out late again. You should talk to him, Joe."

"What am I going to say? He's a grown man."

Benito stopped in the doorway to wave good night, but instead of continuing up the stairs to the bedrooms, he stepped into the kitchen and came to the table and kissed my hand. After that, he did a little dance step out the kitchen door and up the stairs. It all happened so quickly that I didn't know what to say, but Angela said, "Benito is seeing some woman who lives up on the mountain."

"How do you know?" said Joe.

"Mmm, beh, Cristina told me that he bought a box of chocolates at the *tabacchi* store last week. Do you see any chocolates in our house? And the flower man said Benito bought roses last Saturday. Do you see any roses here? And the woman at the —"

"Okay, okay," said Joe. "When the jeweller tells you Benito bought a ring, let me know."

One of the last things we did in the village, before we packed up and headed back to Toronto, was to walk over to Guido and Liounna's house. We timed our visit for four o'clock so they would have already eaten their one o'clock lunch and Guido would have had his afternoon rest, but it would still be a while before the dinner hour. We didn't want Liounna to feel obliged to feed us and we wanted to catch a concert in the village that evening.

Joe had shown us a shortcut to cross the ravine that involved walking through a narrow laneway leading to a parking lot, across the lot, up a set of stairs that belonged to a large six-plex apartment building, and through a short path with a broken gate to the street that wound around to Guido's house. Along this route, we always passed an open garage with dust drifting onto the street — the owner was always in his garage, sanding plaster statues. He'd invited us in one time and we'd admired his plaster sculptures displayed on shelves in his garage. They were a ubiquitous collection of Elvis busts, various archangels in different poses, busts of Caesar and the Pope, a few dwarfs, and several Virgin Marys.

I'd asked Joe about this man, and Joe had said, "That man makes a lotta money. Sells a lotta statues."

"But who buys them?" I asked.

"People," said Joe. "You know, around." And he'd made the circular hand motion. As we passed the garage, Bob made the same gesture. Guido and Liounna's house was the last one on a winding road that held 12 or 15 homes. This was the street, *via piagge*, that my father had lived on when he was a boy and the land was farmland and the homes were little stone cottages with low roofs and cement floors. Although the homes were now large and modern, the grapevines and olive trees were ancient, and Guido and Liounna's house was a one-room stone cottage that they'd put an addition on a dozen years before. So now it was a two-room cottage with a cement driveway larger than the cottage, even though Guido didn't own a car. The house had thick wooden shutters, a cement patio, and a gnarled quince tree in the front, along with the bench my father had bought for Guido a decade before. In the back lived the chickens, beside a vegetable garden and orchard that was tidier than my Toronto house. That's where we expected to find Guido at this time of day, watering his cantaloupes and pepper plants. Instead, we saw a group of strangers standing around a car. A little girl was skipping near the front door, where Liounna was standing, cellphone in hand. She waved the phone and then laughed as she put it back to her ear. "*Scusa*," she said, "Maria and Bob come."

"*Scusa, scusa,*" she continued as she hustled toward us. She looked different somehow. Something more than just the cellphone. Then I realized what it was: Liounna was not wearing her apron. "*Scusa,*" she said once more, and then a string of Italian that Bob and I tried to translate together as she called to the house, "*Guido, vieni. Guido!*"

"I understand that they're going out to a *trattoria*," I said to Bob.

"And they're late," said Bob. "But who are these other people?"

The strangers approached to shake our hands and introduce themselves at the same time that Guido emerged from the house wearing wool trousers and a dress shirt. Liounna was telling him to hurry, and a young woman was trying to corral the skipping girl into the car, where the little boy was standing on the front seat, holding the steering wheel and pretending to drive. In all the confusion, it took me a moment to realize that the man who had introduced himself to us as Guido's oldest son was speaking English.

"We're off to the *trattoria*," he said. "You know the place where the *autostrada* crosses over the road to Ferentino."

"There's a *trattoria* there?" Bob said.

"Yes, of course, the big three-storey house with the green shutters."

"Yes, I know the house," said Bob. "I didn't know it was a *trattoria*."

"Well, there's no sign and I know you Americans like signs," said the son, as if all North Americans had the same affliction. "The food's almost as good as Mama's." He called to Guido, "Ey, Papa, you coming?" and Guido came to shake Bob's hand and explain that they were on their way out.

Then the church bells from San Sebastiano began to ring a low and mournful sound, as if they'd grown heavier and the bell ringer was having difficulty pulling the rope.

"Someone's died," said the son, and he put his hand on his heart.

The little girl stopped skipping, and everyone stood still

for a moment, hands over hearts. Then Guido began to cough, and Liounna opened her handbag and pulled out his puffer. *"Melancholia,"* she said, referring to the sound of the church bells, but she gave a quick glance at Guido and I felt a chill. Guido was well into his 70s and that cough was worrisome. I couldn't imagine a Supino without Guido. He gave me a wink as he got into the car, his eyes the same blue-grey as my father's.

"Prossimo anno," he said.

"Sì, sì," we said. *"Prossimo anno,* see you next year."

We stood in the yard and waved goodbye as if we were the occupants of the little stone cottage and Liounna and Guido were visitors. A brown leaf floated down from the quince tree and landed on the bench. I brushed it away. Bob pulled the gate closed behind us as we began our walk back across the ravine.

"Remember the first time we came to Guido's house and he showed us how you could see the roof of our house across the ravine?"

"You mean, how he took us right into his neighbour's yard across the street and pointed to the roof?" I asked, laughing.

"Exactly. And how the neighbour called out his window at us and when Guido explained who we were, the whole family came out to shake our hands?"

"And we had to have a glass of wine to celebrate?" I said.

"Right. And then we had to try the red wine to compare."

"Yes, and that huge cheese that his wife brought out and sliced?" I said. "And that fabulous bread that was all crusty on the outside and chewy on the inside. I loved that bread."

"All that just to celebrate the view of our new roof," said Bob.

"Let's buy a loaf of that bread tomorrow morning on our way to the airport. If I wrap it up in some of my clothes, it should still be fresh when we get off the plane."

"Do you think you're allowed to take bread on the plane?" asked Bob.

"I don't know, but I'd like the kids to taste it."

"Now," laughed Bob, "who's becoming Italian?"

That evening, a classical music group was scheduled to play in the piazza across from the Church of Santa Maria Maggiore, but when we arrived at eight, there were only white plastic chairs stacked in rows, waiting. We walked down to the *pasticceria* to buy an ice cream — mango and raspberry for me, hazelnut and chocolate for Bob — and then we wandered down to the Kennedy Bar to sit at the new fountain.

We'd been at Guido and Liounna's house, eating home-made pasta at the table set under the quince tree in their front yard, when Guido had first told us they were building a fountain in Supino. He couldn't remember the English word for fountain. "Remember the time I first met you in Rome?" he asked.

"Ten years ago?" asked Bob.

"Really? That long ago? I mean the place."

We'd taken a bus from L'Aquila, where we were staying, into the centre of Rome, and Guido was supposed to meet us at the bus station. He was late, at least by Canadian time standards. And he was supposed to drive us to Supino, but he'd arrived on foot. And he'd taken us by bus to his house. And we'd eaten lunch there and . . .

"You mean the water fountain?" asked Bob.

"Yes!" said Guido. "*Fontana* — they're building one in Supino."

"Where?"

"Where the road grows fat near the Kennedy Bar. In that way, they'll have enough space."

I'd pictured something along the lines of the Trevi Fountain in Rome, where people threw a coin into the water to ensure their return. I imagined tables and chairs scattered here and there on the piazza like the coins sprinkled in the fountain. In Supino, the fountain was built in front of the smallest church in the village, the Church of San Sebastiano. This spot marked the entrance into the village. The fountain was fashioned from cement and resembled a large, flat soup bowl. Instead of a marble statue in the centre, there was a metal pipe where the water would spring like a geyser. Only it didn't. All summer the fountain contained nothing but stray leaves and discarded flyers from the Ferentino Mall. Joe said they were fixing it — something about low water levels and then something about the broken pump, and still the empty bowl sat waiting. The evening of the concert, water gurgled up the metal pipe and cascaded back into the bowl. There was a simplicity about the fountain that almost brought a tear to my eye. The movement of the water produced a slight breeze and children were leaning over the sides, sticking their fingers in the water while mothers warned them not to fall. Because the fountain was built in the middle of the busiest street in the village, cars had to circle the fountain to drive into the village or down to the soccer field.

Bob said, "Joe told me they're going to put a sign right at the bus stop, as you come into the village, saying, 'Drive Slowly.'"

I looked at the cars and motor scooters speeding around the fountain, the men sitting beyond the traffic circle playing cards at the tables outside the Kennedy Bar, and the priest standing in front of San Sebastiano catching the evening breeze. It was chaotic but it was pure Supino, so I rummaged in my purse, pulled out a coin, and tossed it into the fountain. We'd be back next year, renovating a house into a bar, so the coin was more for *buona fortuna* — good luck — than to ensure our return. A blue bus pulled into the square and exhaled diesel fuel and black exhaust and a dozen or more musicians, all dressed in black suits. The driver opened the luggage doors and began to pull out instrument cases. I checked my watch: it was nine o'clock.

"With a little luck," I said, "the concert could begin in half an hour."

We started back up the hill as the musicians starting filing into the Kennedy Bar.

Joe was at the piazza. "The musicians are at the Kennedy Bar," I told him, so Joe began to set up the chairs and Bob helped him. Villagers started arriving in the square. The bar owner put his stereo speaker outside and started playing a medley of Louis Prima songs from the '50s and '60s. Couples began to dance on the cobblestones; children formed a conga line to "*Hey mambo, mambo Italiano.*"

The priest came and sat beside me. "Look at that," he

said, pointing to the bell tower, where the bells were ringing
10 o'clock. "The north star."

By the time the musicians had trouped up the street, the
piazza was full, and by the time they'd set up their music
stands and opened their cases and warmed up their instru-
ments, the bar owner had collected all the scattered espresso
cups and beer glasses and come to lean against the doorway
of his bar. The maestro tapped his baton, the moon peeked
over the bell tower, and the little orchestra began. I searched
the crowd, trying to find Bob, but it was too dark. Beside
me the priest sat with the palms of his hands resting on his
knees, the way my father always sat.

When the song ended, I heard a comforting "Mmmm,"
and Bob's hand was on my shoulder. Everything was okay.

Ten

When we got back to Toronto, Ken met us at the airport. "Dad looks more tired than when he left."

"He's picked up a cough that won't go away. It might have been the dampness."

"Make a doctor's appointment," said Ken.

It was our wedding anniversary and a lot of family were there that day, and after dinner there was an impromptu baseball game on the front lawn. Little Miguel hit the ball with his plastic bat, and Bob picked him up under his arms and ran the bases with him. When they got to third, Bob had a coughing fit and Ken stepped in and ran Miguel home. Bob still couldn't catch his breath.

Our family doctor listened to Bob's lungs and prescribed some cough syrup with codeine. By the second day, the cough had subsided, Bob was feeling better, and we were getting into the busy routine of autumn in Toronto. Kathryn was back at university; Bob was back at the coffee company; my American publisher was arranging a book tour through the northeastern states; and the Supino Social Club was organizing the dinner dance in honour of the feast of some September saint. Bob came home from that meeting in early September and he was coughing again.

"Feel like taking a drive after dinner?" he asked. "One of my customers told me about a second-hand store up near Highway 89 that has an old-fashioned coffee grinder for sale. It's a big one like they used to have on the counter of general stores. I thought it might be good for the bar in Supino. Not to actually grind the coffee, unless the grinder's really precise, but just for the effect, you know."

We drove to the second-hand store. The grinder was solid, with a large wheel and a wooden handle. Bob pulled a handful of roasted coffee beans out of his pocket.

"Does it work?" he asked the storeowner. "Can you adjust the grind?"

The storeowner didn't know, but just as Bob suspected, the grind was too coarse and it was inconsistent.

"It's really just good for display," Bob said, "but I'll take it."

The storeowner helped Bob lift the grinder into the back of the car and, as Bob closed the trunk, he started coughing again.

"Bob," I said.

"I know. I'll call tomorrow."

This time our family doctor sent Bob straight to the

hospital for x-rays. "I'll call you tomorrow as soon as I see the x-rays," the doctor said.

The phone rang at five minutes after nine the next morning.

"I made an appointment for Bob to see the radiologist at the hospital today at 11."

It was September 11. We stopped for gas en route to the hospital and I went inside to pay and to buy Bob another bottle of water. The proprietor had the television on. Some planes had crashed into a tower. When we got to the hospital waiting room, everyone including the medical staff was watching the televisions screens. Bob couldn't concentrate on the magazines or the television. My eyes were on the television, but I couldn't connect to the disaster. I needed all my energy and strength to deal with our own disaster.

This became one of those pivotal moments where people would remember exactly where they were and what they were doing. My reason for remembering September 11 would be different: I'd remember the feeling that I had buried deep under my heart that something was wrong with Bob and that cough that wouldn't go away, but I couldn't think about what it might mean. If I allowed that thought to surface, then a hundred other thoughts would emerge and I'd crumble, as surely as those towers on the television were doing, over and over again. Our 11 o'clock appointment stretched out to noon and then 12:30, and still we hadn't seen the doctor. The nurse was tired of seeing me and I was tired of asking how much longer.

"Let's go," said Bob. "I've waited enough."

"If we leave now, we'll only have to come back again."

Finally, the nurse motioned us into an examining room, where we waited another 10 minutes. Bob sat with his head leaning against the wall and his eyes closed; I paced the small room. At last the doctor walked in, holding the x-rays as if they were heavy sheets of metal. His movements were slow. Again, I thought of those images playing over and over again in slow motion on the television. It seemed as though the world was in shock and everyone and everything was moving slowly. The doctor listened to Bob's chest and said there was definitely some congestion in the lungs. He said that the x-ray was a little blurred and it was difficult to give an exact diagnosis without seeing Bob's medical history.

He said, "When's your next appointment with your oncologist?"

"Next week."

"I'll renew your prescription for the cough syrup. That'll make you more comfortable in the meantime, and I'll send the x-rays down to Princess Margaret. No hurry."

The next week Bob's cough had cleared up, but he asked me to drive to Princess Margaret and let me drop him off at the main door while I went to park the car. Usually we took the stairs to the doctor's office, but that day Bob stopped at the elevator. He walked very slowly down the long hallway to the oncologist's waiting room.

"Give them my name, will you?" Bob said, motioning to the receptionist, and he sat down in the closest chair to catch his breath. In a few minutes, the receptionist called Bob's name and we followed her to the doctor's office. I stood at the oncologist's door, holding it open, waiting for Bob, who was walking slowly so he wouldn't aggravate his cough.

Bob's oncologist pulled the x-rays from their brown manila envelope, put them up on the lightbox, and said, "What the hell happened?"

"You tell us," I said. My heart was pounding in my ears, but I could still hear Bob's laboured breathing.

"I'm sorry, Bob. You can see your whole left lung is grey and your right lung's already beginning to fill with fluid. It's lung cancer and it's pretty advanced."

"Is there anything we can do?" asked Bob.

"No."

Bob reached for my hand. I felt like someone had dropped a cement block on my chest and I was destined to carry that weight for the rest of my life. I heard the doctor's voice, but I couldn't decipher his words.

When Bob stood up, I saw that the doctor was gone. The door was open, and we walked back down the long hallway together. I stopped to phone Kathryn, and then we were in the car driving home. I remember the day in stills, like someone fast-forwarded a movie, stopping here and there.

We were back home sitting on the edge of the bed when Bob finally spoke about the doctor's diagnosis.

"The doctor said the cancer's right through my body. He said there's a sort of web of cancer around my heart. Wouldn't it be funny if I died of a heart attack instead of lung cancer?"

"Oh, Bob. Don't . . ."

"It's going to be okay. I don't want you worrying about

this. There's nothing we can do, but I can say how I live my life until then and it won't be waiting in hospitals and doctors' offices," said Bob. "I want you to do something for me. I don't want to be in a hospital bed, hooked up with tubes and oxygen tanks and machines. I want to be at home with you, and our family. Mmm?" he said.

"Mmm."

Bob was still able to get up and dress every day. We continued with our work routines, but that only lasted a few short weeks. Ken and Kathryn went into the coffee company instead. The next week, they moved our double bed into a room downstairs so Bob wouldn't have to climb the stairs. The room had two windows — one framed the front lawn and the other the long driveway. We placed the bed so Bob could see either view. When he couldn't breathe without help, we arranged for an oxygen tank, but we kept the tank behind the bed.

The end of September marked our youngest grandson Miguel's second birthday. Bob was determined to come to the dinner table. He couldn't make the trip from bedroom to kitchen without his portable oxygen tank. Bob parked the tank behind his chair and tied a balloon on Miguel's chair. "I'm turning off the oxygen when it's time for dessert," he said.

"We don't have to have candles. We can just have cake and ice cream," I said.

"No," said Bob, "let Miguel have his two candles."

That was the last day that Bob was able to come to the dinner table.

Now, the older grandchildren took turns riding the

scooter down the long driveway to get the mail, a trip that
Bob used to make daily with the youngest grandchildren.
They waved to Bob on their way down and waved the mail
on their way back. People sent cards and flowers, but Bob
didn't want them in our room; instead we arranged pictures
of the children and grandchildren and photos of Supino.
We also took the telephone out of the room, putting it in
the kitchen, where I used it, often late at night, sitting on
the floor behind the kitchen door, updating a cousin or a
friend.

Joe called late one night from Supino. "Bloody cancer,"
he said. "Try to be strong, Maria."

Then Davide called to speak with Kathryn, and later with
me. "Maria, *sono* Davide. My father said to tell you he's there
with you and Bob, *ogni momento, ogni giorno*, every moment,
every day."

"Maria, *sono* Liounna. Guido says, *'Mi dispiace, mi dispiace.'*"

We had 42 days together. Bob made a small list of people
he wanted to see one last time. No one stayed long; no one
cried; no one mentioned the reason for the visit, except for
cousin Bill.

He said, "That's got to be a heck of a moment, Bob, to
hear the doctors say they can't do anything."

"One minute I'm making plans in Supino and the next
minute a doctor's giving me a death sentence. Telling me
that it's all over," said Bob. "But I got a few weeks' notice. I
can spend my last days with my family. That's what it comes
down to in the end."

The hospital bed was delivered in October; Bob needed
to sleep in an upright position and we couldn't manage it

properly with pillows. Now I slept on the chesterfield beside the bed. During the day, I spent most of the time sitting on the chair beside the bed. We passed a lot of hours just holding hands. In the evenings, the children and grand-children took turns sitting with Bob and telling him stories of work and school. I spent that time sitting in the living room, reading. I was reading a booklet about death. It listed all the signs of death's approach and I was trying to convince myself that Bob was not showing any of these signs, yet.

I brushed back the curls from his forehead. Bob opened his eyes. "Every time I wake up," he said, "I'm surprised I'm still here."

"I'm glad you're still here," I said.

"I've got something for you. I had given it to Kathryn, to give to you at Christmastime, but I'd like to see you open it."

He reached beneath his pillow and pulled out a small box as dark as a blue Supino sky. Gold letters spelled out the name of the jewellery store. Inside was a pair of gold earrings.

"Oh, Bob, how am I going to live without you?"

"You're strong. You're going to be okay. Tell you what, let's listen to that CD." Bob had bought the soundtrack from *Big Night* and loved that Louie Prima song about the little jewellery shop and the moon above the Mediterranean Sea. "Even though he's singing about Napoli," Bob said, "it reminds me of Supino."

On the Tuesday morning, Bob removed the oxygen tube.

The oxygen dried out his nose and sometimes he liked to have a break from the dryness. I knew that in a few minutes, he'd put it back on. But he didn't.

"You need to keep that on," I reminded him.

"No, I don't. I'm going to die today."

For a moment, I stopped breathing. Had I heard correctly? Was he hallucinating? Was I? The questions flashed through my mind as quickly as shooting stars and all I could grasp were the question marks.

I looked at Ken: he'd heard Bob's words and seemed to be waiting for my response. I wanted to say something positive and comforting, but although Bob's emaciated body was in the room with us, his mind and his soul had already begun to soar.

"No," I said.

"I have to go. He's waiting for me at the gate."

"Who?"

"Your father."

Bob was looking beyond us, as if he could actually see the gate and my father waiting there. I couldn't think of anything to say or do. Bob was so calm, almost joyous. There was no sense of hurry, no glimmer of fear; a peacefulness had settled into the room. Ken was sitting beside the bed, holding his father's hand.

For 42 days and nights, I'd watched helplessly as Bob's body grew weaker, the fluid in his lungs gurgling in the night as he tried to find a space to breathe, his muscles so weak that he couldn't lift the ice chips to his mouth. The oxygen tube was lying on his pillow; if he put it back on, he might breathe a few more minutes, but he was beyond us now, heading somewhere that we could not go. And that somewhere would be peaceful.

I leaned down to kiss Bob's forehead. He spoke so softly. "I'm flying to Italy now. Your father's waiting for me. He's been waiting a long time . . ."

Epilogue

After that first call to Bob's parents, after saying those words, "Bob's dead," I must have called others because my brother and my cousins were at the house. My father-in-law, wearing his sunglasses, was standing in the living room; my cousin Nancy was sitting beside me on the couch, holding my hand. We were drinking whisky and the phone kept ringing.

Some men came from the funeral parlour to pick up Bob's body; our children were all in the bedroom and the men said it might be better if they left, but Kathryn and I stayed. We watched them zip Bob's body into a burgundy plastic body bag — I can still hear the sound of the zipper — and we stood in the doorway and watched them wheel the gurney down the hallway. We heard the sound of the back door closing, the car doors closing, the car heading down the long driveway, and, when we couldn't hear anything more, we went back into the living room to make plans for the next day.

I dressed in black for the funeral-parlour visitation. When I opened the jewellery box to take out the gold earrings Bob had given me, I saw his wedding band nestled there. His fingers had grown so thin that the band kept slipping off and he'd asked me to put it away. Once I'd put on the earrings, it didn't seem right to close up the gold band all alone in the box, so I strung his wedding band on my gold chain and wore it around my neck.

"Ready," said Kathryn. She had the car keys in her hand, but neither of us moved. We knew that once we got into the car, we were beginning a journey that neither of us wanted to take.

We heard a knock on the door. The flower deliveryman stood on our doorstep once again. Kathryn put the small wicker basket stuffed with miniature roses on the kitchen table and pulled out the card: "From your neighbours on *via condotto vecchio.*"

I remembered Peppe's message: "We are with you *ogni momento, ogni giorno*, every moment, every day."

Kathryn and I got into the car. Eight hours later, we were back at the house, and the answering machine was blinking as usual.

"Maria? *Sono* Peppe. *Mi dispiace.* Bob, my friend."

"Maria? *Sono* Liounna. Guido can't speak. *Mi dispiace.*"

"Maria? *Sono* Joe. That bloody cancer. The neighbours ask me to phone and say *mi dispiace.*"

"Maria," said the president of the Supino Social Club. "Everyone is welcome to come to the club after the funeral on Saturday. We'll take care of the food. Your brother phoned and offered to pay for the drinks, but I told him, 'For Bob McLean, we take care of everything. Son of Supino, you understand?'"

Months passed. I thought about selling the little house in Supino, but I couldn't do that without solving the hydro issue and the constantly disappearing patio. We might have a terra cotta patio now; Bob would never see it.

"We should plan our trip to Supino," said Kathryn.

"I don't want to go. I can't bear the idea of seeing Guido and Joe and Peppe and all of them. They'll all want to say sorry and shake my hand."

"What's wrong with that? You'd be pretty upset if they didn't want to."

"That's the thing. I don't want them to say sorry, and I don't want them to say nothing, so I don't want to go."

"I think that's a little crazy, Mom."

"Me too."

But my life *was* a little crazy. The original shock had worn off, and I was hanging on to an idea that I'd read and heard over and over again: that if you could get through the first year, things got easier. Peppe had sent a Christmas card that year, and inside he'd written a note, assuring me that, in time, I'd remember only the good memories. Since Peppe's wife had died of cancer years ago, I believed him, and I tried to hold on to the good memories. But somehow those good memories were the very thing that kept me from wanting to return to the village. I tried to imagine myself in Supino without Bob. Would I walk down to the Bar Italia every morning by myself? Bianca would have to reach for one cup, instead of two. I'd have to try not to cry.

Then my friend Netta called me one day. She works in publicity and marketing.

"Jeanne Marshall from the *National Post* wants to do an interview with you."

"I've cancelled all my book publicity stuff," I said.

"I know, but Jeanne's currently living in Rome and would like to do the interview there. I figured you could do it en route to Supino."

"I'm not going to Supino."

"Why not? Supino's always good for you."

"Let me think about it."

"You should go," said Kathryn when I told her about the call. "I can drive us into Rome from the airport, you can do the interview. We'll stay overnight and drive down to Supino the next day."

A decade before, when we'd bought the house, Bob had said that we'd always have it as a part of my father's village and our village. Now I'd have to see Supino as *my* village, if I could. I began to visualize myself alone in Supino, but I was never alone. The memory of my father, the memory of Bob, all the good memories accompanied me. I imagined the villagers still watching out for my little house, and me. When the president of the Supino Social Club called me to talk about the proposed *National Post* interview in Rome, I never even considered how he knew about it.

"After the interview in Rome," he began, "we want to make a little *festa* in the village. Father Antonio will bless the book. Will you donate a signed copy for the Supino library? Afterwards, we'll have a little dinner at the restaurant in the woods. The journalist can be the guest of honour. Bring the photographer. We'll make them honorary Supino Social Club members. What's the date of the interview, Maria?"

In the end, a letter from Sergio Coletta in Moss Point, Mississippi, helped me to decide. He wrote that he remembered that this was the time of year when Bob and I would be planning our trip to Supino:

> Thank you for the cedar branch that you sent with your letter. You have no idea how much that meant to me. You're very kind. Maybe I can do something for you. I don't know if you stop in Rome when you go to Supino, but my son-in-law's cousin owns a small hotel and restaurant in Rome near the Vatican and I am sending his business card. They are looking forward to meeting you.

In Supino, there's a question our neighbours often ask — a kind of Supinese version of "How are things going?" *Tutto a posto?* literally means *Is everything in place?* And so it seemed that everything was in place that summer for me to return to the village. I found myself sitting in the departure lounge at the Toronto airport. Once we landed in Rome and picked up our rental car, I'd meet the journalist at Osteria dei Pontefici, Sergio Coletta's son-in-law's cousin's restaurant in Rome, and the following day we'd head down the *autostrada* until we reached the blue sign pointing to Supino.

The news of Bob's death would have rung from the bell tower of San Sebastiano and sprung from the fountain in a hundred icy teardrops. The wind would have already carried his name beyond the village and up the mountain path to Santa Serena to put down roots among the clouds. The village would open her arms to me, and I would walk right into them, as if I had come home.

Acknowledgements

Thank you to the wonderful villagers in Supino and from Supino (now scattered across the globe) for your fine hospitality and your interest in *My Father Came from Italy* and in *Summers in Supino: Becoming Italian*.

I'm grateful to have Carolyn Swayze as my agent and my friend, and to work with Jack David and his talented team at ECW Press.

My thanks to early readers Maria Cioni, Janet Looker, and Kathryn McLean. And to Johnny and Suzy Paglia, who provided the Italian translations.

Most of all I wish to thank my children Rob, Ken, Carole, Paula, and Kathryn, and their partners and my grandchildren, especially Paige and Miguel, who shared the difficult days of Bob's illness with me. Every family member contributed in their own way even though they are not mentioned individually in the book, and every one of them, including the newest grandson, Julian Robert, remain the most important blessings of my life, as they were of Bob's.

Get the
eBook Free!
*Proof of Purchase
Required*

At ECW Press, we want you to enjoy this book in whatever format you like, whenever you like. Leave your print book at home and take the eBook to go! Purchase the print edition and receive the eBook free. Just send an email to ebook@ecwpress.com and include:

· the book title
· the name of the store where you purchased it
· your receipt number
· your preference of file type: PDF or ePub?

A real person will respond to your email with your eBook attached. And thanks for supporting an independently owned Canadian publisher with your purchase!